THEY HAD A DREAM

"Agitate! Agitate! Agitate!"
—Frederick Douglass (1817?–1895)
The civil rights struggle in the United States occurred in three stages. In the first stage, blacks kidnapped from Africa and made slaves in America struggled for freedom. The charismatic figure of that movement was Frederick Douglass.

"Where is the black man's government?"—Marcus Garvey
(1887–1940)
The second stage occurred after the Civil War, when freed slaves struggled to surmount prejudice and persecution. The black leader who developed black nationalism and black pride was Marcus Garvey.

"I have a dream." *—Martin Luther King, Jr. (1929–1968)*
The third movement began in the 1960s, when a strong civil rights movement forged ahead in two divergent directions. The Reverend Martin Luther King, Jr., organized a powerful nonviolent civil disobedience movement to win equal rights through integration.

"I don't advocate violence, but..."—Malcolm X (1925–1965)
In contrast, until the last years of his life Malcolm X sought equal rights for blacks through violent confrontation and through racial separation.

OTHER PUFFIN TITLES OF
HISTORY AND BIOGRAPHY

EPOCH BIOGRAPHIES

They Had a Dream

The Civil Rights Struggle
from Frederick Douglass
to Marcus Garvey
to Martin Luther King
and Malcolm X

JULES ARCHER

PUFFIN BOOKS

PUFFIN BOOKS
Published by the Penguin Group
Penguin Books USA Inc., 375 Hudson Street, New York, New York 10014, U.S.A.
Penguin Books Ltd, 27 Wrights Lane, London W8 5TZ, England
Penguin Books Australia Ltd, Ringwood, Victoria, Australia
Penguin Books Canada Ltd, 10 Alcorn Avenue, Toronto, Ontario, Canada M4V 3B2
Penguin Books (N.Z.) Ltd, 182–190 Wairau Road, Auckland 10, New Zealand

Penguin Books Ltd, Registered Offices: Harmondsworth, Middlesex, England

First published in the United States of America by Viking,
a division of Penguin Books USA Inc., 1993
Published in Puffin Books, 1996

9 10

Series created by Lucas Evans Books, Inc.
Photograph of Frederick Douglass on cover: University of Chicago Library,
Department of Special Collections.

THE LIBRARY OF CONGRESS HAS CATALOGED THE VIKING EDITION AS FOLLOWS:
Archer, Jules. They had a dream: the civil rights struggle, from Frederick Douglass
to Marcus Garvey to Martin Luther King, Jr., and Malcolm X / Jules Archer.
p.   cm.—(Epoch biographies)
Summary: Traces the progression of the civil rights movement and its effect on
history through biographical sketches of four prominent and influential
African-Americans: Frederick Douglass, Marcus Garvey,
Martin Luther King, Jr., and Malcolm X.
ISBN 0-670-84494-2
1. Civil rights workers—United States—Biography—Juvenile literature.
2. Douglass, Frederick, 1817?–1895—Juvenile literature. 3. Garvey, Marcus,
1887–1940—Juvenile literature. 4. King, Martin Luther, Jr., 1929–1968—
Juvenile literature. 5. X, Malcolm, 1925–1965—Juvenile literature. 6. Afro-
Americans—Civil rights—History—Juvenile literature. 7. Civil rights move-
ments—United States—History—Juvenile literature. [1. Civil rights workers.
2. Afro-Americans—Biography. 3. Civil rights movements—History.] I. Title.
II. Series.
E185.96.A73   1993 323'.092'273—dc20 [B] 92-40071 CIP AC

Puffin Books ISBN 0-14-034954-5

Printed in the United States of America

Dedicated with love

to my sons
(in alphabetical order this time)

Dr. Dane Archer
of Santa Cruz, California

Dr. Kerry Russell Archer
of Boxford, Massachusetts

Dr. Michael Archer
of Randwick, Australia

and to
Dorothy "Sunny" Soulé

CONTENTS

INTRODUCTION

J U S T before the Japanese attack on Pearl Harbor, I was drafted and sent to Camp Croft in South Carolina from my home in New York City. In Spartanburg I was astonished and disturbed to see local blacks step off the sidewalk into the gutter to allow white people to pass.

Months later, in a New Guinea jungle during World War II, I was given a lift in a jeep by a black GI. I told him what I had seen in Spartanburg. Why, I asked, did southern blacks feel the need to be so cowed and deferential toward whites? I never forgot his reply.

"Just let the white man drop his whip," he said with a grim smile, "and then watch what happens!"

The civil rights struggle in the United States occurred in three stages. In the first stage blacks kidnapped from Africa and made slaves in America struggled for freedom. The charismatic figure of that movement was Frederick Douglass (1817?–1895).

The second stage occurred after the Civil War when freed slaves struggled to surmount prejudice and persecution, a period lasting a century. The black leader who defied discrimination with an inseminating movement that developed black nationalism and black pride was Marcus Garvey (1887–1940).

The third stage began in the 1960s, when a strong civil rights movement forged ahead in two divergent directions. The Reverend Martin Luther King, Jr., (1929–1968) organized a powerful nonviolent civil disobedience movement to win equal rights through integration. He was supported by millions of whites who believed in social justice. In contrast, Malcolm X (1925–1965) sought equal rights for blacks through violent confrontation and through racial separation.

The civil rights struggle can best be perceived and understood through the lives and works of these four outstanding black leaders in American history. Each significantly influenced and changed the direction of that struggle. Yet except for Martin Luther King, they are relatively neglected in histories written by, for, and about whites.

"The obscurity of these freedom fighters," observes white historian George Levesque, "suggests how invisible blacks can be to whites."

These "invisible" people have been known by several names over the centuries. First they were called Negroes, then coloreds, then blacks, and now some prefer the term Afro-Americans or African Americans. However, for the purposes of this book, the term *blacks* has been used as the one preferred by the subjects of my biographies, and by most contemporary blacks themselves.

I wish to express my gratitude for the cooperation of Benjamin L. Hooks, executive director/CEO of the National Association for the Advancement of Colored People; John J. Jacobs, president/CEO of the National Urban League, Inc.; Bobby Seale, cofounder of the Black Panthers; and David Hilliard, former Black Panther chief-of-staff.

My purpose in writing this book is to help white readers understand the story of the black struggle in America as they may never have known it before and to help black readers appreciate fully their proud and remarkable heritage.

Jules Archer
Santa Cruz, California

They Had a Dream

The
History
of the
Black Struggle
in America

ONE

S I N C E ancient times, racial prejudice has been used to justify slavery. It was the justification in America when the first twenty Africans were imported into Virginia as bound servants in 1619. British writers defended slavery as "the Backbone and mainspring of British commerce," calling the kidnapped Africans "ignoble savages."

While slavery flourished openly in American colonies, the possibility of slave revolts was a constant fear. Many colonies forbade blacks to assemble, travel without permission, bear arms, or possess liquor. In Virginia any master who killed his slave for "resisting correction" went free on the assumption he would not destroy his own valuable property without just cause.

One of the earliest slave revolts took place in New York City in 1712. Eight thousand whites owned two thousand slaves, most of whom were cruelly treated. Gathering secretly after midnight, twenty-three slaves set fire to a house as a signal to the city's blacks that an uprising had begun. Armed with guns, long knives, and hatchets they had secured from drunken crews in port, they attacked whites, killing nine.

The governor's soldiers routed and pursued them. Some trapped slaves turned guns and knives on themselves rather than be captured. Twenty-one were executed; some hanged, some tortured and broken on the wheel, some burned to death. This cycle of cruel treatment, revolt, and violent suppression would be repeated throughout slavery's existence in America.

By 1760 almost half a million slaves were working on southern plantations. Thomas Jefferson himself was a slaveholder who saw no possibility that blacks and whites could ever live together as equals. In 1776 he warned that Americans would one day pay bitterly for having brought the black man to this continent in chains, and urged resettling slaves in Africa.

His views underwent change four years later, however, when he advocated total emancipation. Some said the reason was his affair with a black slave and their five children. But 1801 was also when a slave insurrection broke out in Virginia and some thirty-five black rebels were executed. A gloomy Jefferson prophesied, "We are truly to be pitied. . . . I tremble for my country when I reflect that God is just." He sought to trouble the conscience of fellow Virginians by reminding them, "One *day* of American slavery is worse than a *thousand years* of what we rose in arms to oppose!"

At Jefferson's insistence, Congress passed the Act to Prohibit the Importation of Slaves after 1808. This law, however, did not stop an illegal slave traffic. It continued to flourish until the Civil War, earning fat profits for northern shipowners.

Slavery also earned huge profits for southern plantation owners, thanks to Eli Whitney's cotton gin, invented in 1793. With the problem of processing the plant solved, the cotton industry grew rapidly, as did the need for slave field hands on the plantations. Significantly, 1793 was also the year Congress passed the first Fugitive Slave Law, levying a $500 fine on anyone attempting to conceal or rescue an escaped slave.

But this did nothing to stop slaves' resistance. By 1820 there had been over 250 slave revolts. The largest occurred in 1811, when a slave named Charles led five hundred slaves in a revolt at the Andre sugar plantation north of New Orleans. After wounding Andre and killing his son, they seized arms and advanced down the coast, smashing and looting property. Terrified whites fled before them.

In a battle with several hundred U.S. troops and militia, eighty-three slaves were killed. Sixteen were arrested, tried, and executed. Their heads were mounted on poles at intervals along the Mississippi River as a grim warning to all restless slaves.

T W O

T H E R E was now growing support in the North for solving the "black problem" by resettling free blacks in African colonies. Paul Cuffee, a Boston Quaker, took one shipload of black passengers to settle in Sierra Leone. In 1816 the American Colonization Society (ACS) was founded to promote the plan, in the belief that blacks were a troublesome minority best gotten rid of. Prominent members included James Madison, Andrew Jackson, Daniel Webster, Stephen Douglas, and James Monroe. Congress supported the ACS, authorizing money to transport twenty thousand free blacks to establish an African colony, which became Liberia.

By 1819 there was an even balance between northern states that barred slavery and southern states that depended on it. As the friction between them grew more intense, a northern abolitionist movement sprang up. Abolitionists created what was called the Underground Railroad, an escape route to Canada for runaway slaves. Escapees were hunted by "slavecatchers" who were paid bounties for each runaway captured.

Despite these dangers, as many as twenty thousand slaves escaped on the Underground Railroad before the Civil War. Some returned to the South to serve as guides for other escapees. The most famous of these was Harriet Tubman, who carried a $10,000 bounty for her capture—dead or alive.

Meanwhile, the slave revolts continued. In 1822, an informer revealed a plot by a free Haitian black, Denmark Vesey, to lead an uprising of all blacks in South Carolina. The plot was quickly crushed, and thirty-seven blacks were executed.

A black Boston ragman, David Walker, published a pamphlet called *Walker's Appeal* in 1830, calling upon all southern slaves to revolt. Copies found their way below the Mason-Dixon line, the informal boundary between slave and free states, leading southern port police to search ships for the incendiary pamphlet. Any black seaman found with one was jailed and flogged.

One year later fresh panic swept the South. Nat Turner, a thirty-one-year-old Virginia slave, had awed fellow slaves with his report of hearing "a loud noise in the heavens," followed by the appearance of a spirit who revealed that he had been chosen by God to lead the slaves out of bondage. With his disciples Turner plotted a swift and terrible massacre that would terrify whites into fleeing before them. He and five slaves murdered their sleeping master, his wife, and three children. Seizing guns and ammunition, they sped from plantation to plantation, gathering sixty-four more recruits.

In each house the mob burst into, they assassinated all white occupants and seized muskets, axes, scythes, swords, and clubs. In two days, over fifty-seven white men, women, and children were slain in a twenty-mile area. Word flashed around the countryside, then all through the South.

"The slaves are plotting! The Negroes have risen!"

Military forces swept through the county, killing over a hundred slaves indiscriminately in a vengeful massacre. Many of Turner's followers were captured and killed on the spot; some were decapitated. Nineteen were tried and executed. Nat Turner was hanged.

Turner's rebellion sent shivers up and down the spines of

all southerners. "It is like a smothered volcano," quavered
Mrs. Lawrence Lewis, George Washington's niece. "We know
not when, or where, the flame will burst forth, but we know
that death in the most repulsive form awaits us."

Infuriated slaveowners blamed David Walker's pamphlet
and the agitation of the North's most militant and active
abolitionist, William Lloyd Garrison. Garrison had begun publishing an abolitionist newspaper, *The Liberator*, in 1831. In
the following year he organized the New England Anti-Slavery
Society (NEASS) with a merchant colleague, Lewis Tappan.
Through his paper and the NEASS, Garrison not only condemned the southern system of slavery, but he also accused
New Englanders of hypocrisy for professing to oppose slavery
while using products produced by the slave states.

Garrison demanded in his paper that northerners boycott
slave-produced products. But many northern businessmen
had investments in southern plantations or traded with them.
One New York businessman told abolitionist minister
Samuel J. May, "It is a matter of business necessity. We cannot afford to let you succeed."

Some northern newspapers denounced the abolitionists
for holding integrated meetings, and accused them of fostering
intermarriage. Northern racist mobs staged proslavery riots
during the summer of 1834 in New York, New Jersey, Pennsylvania, Connecticut, Ohio, and Michigan.

Garrison himself received hundreds of letters threatening
his life. When he tried to speak at the Boston Female Anti-
Slavery Society in 1835, he was seized by a mob and led
through the streets by a rope around his neck. He had to be
rescued by burly truckers sent to his aid by Boston's mayor.

In the South, meanwhile, slaveowner brutality grew increasingly savage. In Tennessee a slave who had fought back

and killed a cruel master was burned alive over a slow fire before a crowd of thousands. One minister criticized the punishment; he would have preferred the slave be torn to pieces wih red-hot pincers.

"This," Garrison asked in horror, "is a man of God?"

Garrison was joined in his abolitionist crusade by escaped slave Frederick Douglass, who moved audiences with his own story of suffering at the hands of cruel slave masters. While rallying the conscience of white Americans with Garrison, Douglass also encouraged freed blacks to enter the political struggle against slavery through his newspaper *The North Star*. Throughout the Civil War and the fight for black freedom that followed, Douglass would be the leading black spokesman for racial equality.

THREE

THE westward expansion of America intensified the struggle between North and South over the political balance of slave and free states. Congress stirred a northern furor by passing the Fugitive Slave Act of 1850, providing federal aid in apprehending runaways and punishing anyone hindering their recapture, whether they were in a free territory or not.

That fury was seen in full force in 1854, when Anthony Burns, a runaway slave from Virginia, was arrested in Boston on a fugitive slave warrant. Outraged abolitionists aroused a crowd of fifty thousand to attempt an unsuccessful rescue of Burns from his prison cell. It took a thousand soldiers and police with drawn guns to force the prisoner aboard a ship sailing for Virginia.

Like Congress, the Supreme Court took a dim view of the rights of all blacks. In the *Dred Scott* decision of 1857, Chief Justice Roger Taney declared that no slave or descendant could be a U.S. citizen and Congress had no right to prohibit slavery in the territories because it deprived southerners of slave "property" without due process of law.

With the presidential election of 1860 approaching, slavery was a much-debated issue. But there was basic agreement between the two candidates for the Republican nomination. Both Stephen Douglas and Abraham Lincoln favored the forced emigration of blacks. Lincoln also believed that blacks were mentally and morally inferior to whites and conceded to Douglas that federal power should not infringe upon states' rights to slavery.

Lincoln was nominated by the Republicans in May 1860 under voting rules that allowed freed blacks to vote in only five northern states. Abolitionist Wendell Phillips responded with a slashing editorial in Garrison's *Liberator* assailing him as "the Slave Hound of Illinois."

When the Civil War broke out on April 12, 1861, after Lincoln's election, many whites in northern and border states angrily blamed blacks in their midst. As law enforcement officials looked the other way, white mobs attacked black communities in Memphis, Louisville, Cincinnati, and Detroit. To pacify whites in the border states, the Union army was given strict orders not to interfere with slavery there.

At first the Union army refused to enlist free blacks. Eventually, however, 156,000 black troops were accepted. Fighting thirty-nine major battles, they earned Congressional Medals of Honor, despite treatment inferior to that accorded white troops.

Lincoln was fearful that millions of northerners who were fighting and financing a war to hold the Union together would balk at doing so to abolish slavery. Emancipation, he worried, would also drive the border states into the arms of the South.

He stated, "My paramount object is to save the Union, and not either to save or destroy slavery. . . . If I could save the Union without freeing any slaves, I would do it."

Finally, however, he felt reluctantly driven to issue the Emancipation Proclamation on January 1, 1863. Even then, it was more a war strategy than a moral document. It only freed slaves in the Confederacy, in the hope that they would desert southern plantations for Union lines. Slaves in border states or in southern areas under Union control remained the property of whites. It would take almost three years before slavery would be completely abolished under the Thirteenth Amendment, adopted on December 18, 1865.

In the North, the Emancipation Proclamation stirred a white backlash. In March antiblack riots broke out in Detroit. Three months later New York saw a series of antidraft riots, during which blacks were hanged from lampposts by mobs of poor white laborers. They were furious at a draft law that permitted rich men to pay other people to serve in their places, and at freed slaves brought north for use as strikebreakers.

Southerners reacted to the Emancipation Proclamation with disbelief and horror. The Presbyterian church of the South went so far as to pass a resolution declaring slavery to be a divine institution ordained by God.

The end of the Civil War on April 9, 1865, did nothing to change antiblack sentiment in either the North or South. Five days after the southern surrender, President Lincoln was assassinated. The New York City Council, fearing another wave of antiblack riots, refused to allow blacks to march in the funeral procession. In the South, slavery was simply replaced by a new system of black bondage.

FOUR

WHILE blacks were no longer legally bound to southern plantations, sharecropping fulfilled the same purpose. Former slaves now rented farmland from white landlords. The rents were set so high that blacks could never pay them off from the produce they grew. They were thus caught in a spiraling debt that kept them impoverished and undernourished. "Black Codes," racist regulations passed by the white ruling class, further bound freed slaves to white landlords.

Southerners also used a variety of ruses to keep blacks from voting. Blacks who tried to vote were refused ballots because they didn't have grandfathers who'd voted, or hadn't paid a poll tax they couldn't afford, or couldn't pass a difficult literacy test given only to blacks, or hadn't voted in a primary election open only to whites.

Lincoln's successor, President Andrew Johnson, was more concerned with how to help the bankrupt South than with helping the four million freed slaves. A former southern slave-owner, Johnson argued that blacks, only one in ten of whom could read or write, were not equipped to act as "lawgivers for a great nation" because they simply had no "capacity for so high a function." He objected to blacks serving on juries judging white defendants, calling this both unconstitutional and "insulting to the white mass of Americans." Instead of civil rights laws, Johnson asked Congress for measures to help the southern states recover.

Congress angrily refused. If the Rebels were to be rewarded instead of punished, what, then, had the war been all about? Overriding President Johnson's veto, they created a Freedmen's Bureau to combat the southern Black Codes. This measure helped former slaves by giving them land and by trying anyone accused of depriving them of their new civil rights in army courts.

In April 1866 Congress also passed a Civil Rights Act conferring U.S. citizenship on freed blacks and making it a federal misdemeanor to violate their rights. Further, Congress clamped tighter controls on the South with four Reconstruction Acts. All these measures were backed by federal troops stationed in the South, and all were passed over President Johnson's veto.

The result of these acts, however, was to turn control of the South over to northern business interests. Backed by the bayonets of federal troops, state governments were soon run by white "carpetbaggers" and their black puppets. Predictably, white southerners reacted with violence.

A drive to expel Reconstruction officials and suppress the freed blacks was spearheaded by the Ku Klux Klan, first organized in Pulaski, Tennessee, in 1866. Employing threats and mob violence, hooded Klansmen united masses of white southerners behind their crusade, especially lower-class workers who feared the competition of free black labor. The Klan frightened blacks into staying away from election polls by burning crosses and flogging and torturing freedmen. Those who resisted were lynched.

In angry reply to southern violence, Congress passed the Fourteenth Amendment guaranteeing full citizenship to all persons born in the United States. It prevented any state from passing a law to deprive any citizen of life, liberty, or property, guaranteeing all "equal protection of the laws."

Under the administration of President Grant, elected in 1868 with strong black support, the federal government continued to support black rights. Grant won ratification of the Fifteenth Amendment strengthening black suffrage, and executed the Enforcement Act of 1870 to empower it. In 1871 he became a hero to blacks by ordering the Ku Klux Klan disbanded. Hundreds of Klansmen were arrested under an act of Congress.

However, this act was later overturned. That same year the Supreme Court undermined the Fifteenth Amendment, declaring that it did not prevent "the deprivation of [citizens'] common rights by state legislation." This cruel decision left southern blacks to the mercies of state and local officials.

How merciful they would be was suggested by an editorial in the *Atlanta News* responding to President Grant's proposal for a new civil rights bill: "Let there be White Leagues formed in every town, village and hamlet of the South, and let us organize for the great struggle which seems inevitable. . . . [I]t is time to meet brute-force with brute-force. . . . Act the moment Grant signs the civil rights bill [which is] a declaration of war against Southern whites."

F I V E

IN 1875 Grant sent his civil rights bill to Congress, which guaranteed blacks equal rights in public places and forbade their exclusion from juries. Despite bitter opposition from white southern congressmen, the bill passed, only to be declared unconstitutional by a hostile Supreme Court.

Meanwhile, White Leagues were springing up throughout the South, directing mob riots against black officials and white Radical Republicans. Their war against Reconstruction was aided in 1876, when Rutherford B. Hayes won the tight presidential election through fraud committed by three southern canvassing boards. He promptly repaid them by beginning to withdraw federal troops from the South.

Hayes assured the country that this action was a "much

needed measure for the restitution of local self-government
and the promotion of national harmony." But with their protection by federal forces now gone, blacks saw their hard-won
freedoms quickly eroded. Southern legislatures were soon re-
captured from the Radical Republicans. Lynchings and mob
violence continued without opposition. And Jim Crow laws
and the unwritten prewar code of black behavior again controlled blacks' daily lives.

Under this code, every encounter between a black person
and a southern white became a lesson in black inferiority.
Whites had to be addressed as Mr., Marse, or Miss. Blacks
were simply called "boy" or "girl" or referred to by their first
name only. Blacks could not shake a white man's hand, call
on a white man's house at the front door, or eat at a white
man's table. If a black encountered a white person on a narrow
sidewalk, he had to step into the gutter to let the white pass.

By the end of the nineteenth century, the Fourteenth and
Fifteenth Amendments had become dead-letter laws in southern states. While 67 percent of blacks had registered to vote
in 1867, only 6 percent dared register in 1882, when the last
federal troops were withdrawn from the South. Mob violence
and lynchings—over two thousand in the last two decades of
the century alone—crushed black resistance.

Under the constant oppression and violence, blacks began
to flee the South in large numbers. Between 1879 and 1890,
fifty thousand black sharecroppers migrated to the West and
Midwest. More blacks went north in search of factory work.

Prejudiced northerners responded by adopting Jim Crow
customs of their own. The problem was particularly acute in
northern cities, where blacks soon found themselves barred
from restaurants, theaters, hotels, and stores.

In 1895 Homer Plessy, a one-eighth black, sat down in a

Louisiana "whites only" railroad car to challenge that state's segregation policies. He believed the Fourteenth Amendment would protect him. But when *Plessy v. Ferguson* reached the Supreme Court, the court ruled that all any state had to do was provide "separate but equal" facilities for blacks. It added an arrogant insult: "If one race be inferior to the other socially, the Constitution of the United States cannot put them on the same plane."

A rejoicing South used this decision to justify segregation for the next fifty-eight years.

Segregation was quickly extended to cover every area of black life. Blacks could not eat with whites, play in the same parks as whites, or attend the same schools. Oklahoma went as far as segregating its phone books. Segregation even continued after death, with separate cemeteries for blacks and whites.

Theodore Roosevelt, who was elected president in 1900, expressed the attitudes of most white Americans. When vice president, he wrote, "As a race . . . the [blacks] are altogether inferior to the whites. . . . A perfectly stupid race can never rise to a very high place. . . . I do not believe that the average Negro . . . is as yet in any way fit to take care of himself and others. . . . If he were, there would be no Negro race problem."

But even Roosevelt underestimated the level of racial hatred in the South. In 1901 he invited Booker T. Washington, the founder of the first college for blacks, Tuskegee Institute, to lunch at the White House. The South approved of Washington's emphasis on black responsibility rather than rights, but this was too much. South Carolina Senator "Pitchfork Ben" Tillman expressed southern sentiment: "The action of President Roosevelt entertaining that nigger will necessitate our killing a thousand niggers in the South before they will learn their place again."

Black sociologist William Du Bois challenged both whites' Jim Crow laws and the "accommodationist" policies of Booker T. Washington, who was then the leading spokesman for black rights. With other black leaders Du Bois founded the Niagara Movement in 1906. "We refuse to allow the impression to remain," they stated, "that the Negro-American assents to inferiority, is submissive under oppression and apologetic before insults. . . . The voice of ten million Americans must never cease to assail the ears of their fellows, as long as America is unjust."

Three years later the Niagara Movement became the National Association for the Advancement of Colored People (NAACP). For the rest of the century, it would lead the legal battle to end discrimination, segregation, voting restrictions, and violence against blacks.

When Woodrow Wilson was elected president in 1912, he promised "fair and just treatment for all." But for the native Virginian, "all" did not include blacks, whom he referred to during his professorship at Princeton as "unschooled in self-control . . . insolent and aggressive; sick of work, covetous of pleasure." Wilson segregated the Post Office and Treasury Department, professing this would "reduce friction."

All through the first part of the twentieth century, the cause of black rights met resistance from every branch of the government. Even the fledgling film industry joined the antiblack majority. In 1915, race prejudice in America was inflamed by director D. W. Griffith's film *The Birth of a Nation*. Based on Thomas Dixon, Jr.'s 1905 novel *The Clansman*, it glorified the Ku Klux Klan as noble defenders of white civilization against a "black reign of terror," an image the Klan would use to recruit new members in the 1920s.

But while blacks in America remained segregated from whites, discriminated against, and subject to terror by vigilante groups, a looming international conflict was about to give them their first glimpse of a world where equality seemed possible.

S I X

W H E N World War I broke out in Europe, masses of southern blacks migrated north for work in the booming defense industries. They were greeted by race riots and bombings targeted against black families who moved into white neighborhoods.

Two new organizations were formed to deal with the crisis in the cities. In 1910 the National Urban League was founded to help southern blacks—nearly two million of whom moved north between 1910 and 1940—adjust to city life. The Urban League helped them find jobs, fostered black health and education, and sought to prevent delinquency.

In 1916 Jamaican immigrant Marcus Garvey moved the headquarters of his Universal Negro Improvement Association (UNIA) to New York City. While the Urban League sought to integrate blacks into white society, Garvey took a separatist approach, organizing a "back to Africa" movement that attracted a hundred thousand members. His emphasis on black pride, expressed in the motto "Black Is Beautiful," inspired thousands of blacks and would later give rise to a movement to win blacks control of their urban neighborhoods.

Meanwhile, 350,000 blacks from across the country joined the Army, and many of them served overseas. The Army was segregated, and the Navy and Marines barred blacks from service. Yet, serving abroad, thousands of blacks experienced equal treatment from whites for the first time. When these veterans returned home, some decorated as war heroes, they felt that they had earned the right to equal and unsegregated treatment from the country they had fought for.

What they found instead was increased racial tension and violence. The riots in the cities and industrial competition from blacks had led to renewed growth and activity for the Klan in both the North and South. By 1925 the Klan had some five million members and control of legislatures in Colorado, Texas, Oklahoma, Louisiana, Maine, and Kansas. Blacks in uniform were a particular target of Klansmen in the South, where seventy-eight black veterans were lynched.

Lynching had been employed by racists to terrorize blacks into submission since before the Civil War. Black teacher Ida B. Wells first brought this disgrace to public attention in 1884, when she launched a one-woman crusade against the practice. Now the NAACP took up the cause, demanding that the federal government take action. They received the same response that Ida Wells had received almost forty years earlier: lynching was a state matter and the U.S. government would not interfere.

President Franklin D. Roosevelt, whose election in 1933 had wholehearted black support, publicly condemned lynching. But when NAACP executive secretary Walter White asked him to support an anti-lynching bill in 1938, FDR refused for fear of alienating southern congressmen. The bill was stopped by a southern filibuster.

Southern lynching persisted without interruption into the 1960s.

However, President Roosevelt's "New Deal" administration did bring some benefits to blacks. In 1936 the president

established a "Black Cabinet" composed of black businessmen and political leaders to advise and assist him in obtaining
equal rights for blacks. The sole woman selected was Mary
McLeod Bethune, founder of the eminent coed Bethune-
Cookman College, whom Roosevelt named director of Negro
affairs for his National Youth Administration.

In 1938 Roosevelt created a Civil Rights Section in the
Justice Department to enforce the rights of southern blacks.
Blacks also benefited economically from the social welfare
programs designed to combat the Great Depression that now
affected all Americans.

Crisis, the newspaper of the NAACP, summed up the
New Deal for blacks in 1940: "[The] most important contri-
bution of the Roosevelt Administration to the age-old color-
line problem in America has been its doctrine that Negroes
are a part of the country and must be considered in any program for the country as a whole. . . . For the first time in their
lives, government has taken on meaning and substance for
the Negro masses."

In the early 1940s Swedish sociologist Gunnar Myrdal and
Ralph Bunche, then a professor at black Howard University,
traveled through the South interviewing blacks and whites
for a study of prejudice in America. They were pursued by a
mob of "rednecks" and barely escaped with their lives. Their
investigation resulted in Myrdal's *An American Dilemma*,
published in 1944, one of the classic studies of the underlying
causes of racial violence and bigotry. But it was Bunche's
words written to Myrdal before their investigation that expressed the growing rage felt by many blacks: "There are
Negroes . . . who, fed up with frustration of their life here, see
no hope and express an angry desire 'to shoot their way out

of it.' I have on many occasion heard Negroes exclaim, 'Just give us machine guns and we'll blow the lid off the whole damn business.' "

S E V E N

WHEN World War II broke out in Europe, blacks again sought jobs in the northern defense industry. And again they ran into a wall of discrimination.

Under pressure from black leaders, President Roosevelt quickly established a Fair Employment Practices Committee (FEPC). The FEPC was strongly opposed in many northern communities and violently challenged throughout the South. But black employment in defense industries did increase significantly, as any firm found to be practicing discrimination was denied war production contracts.

Race riots again broke out in the cities. One of the worst in American history occurred in 1942 in Detroit, a city filled with recently arrived white and black southerners. When they were crowded together in slums and tent and trailer camps, tempers reached flash point. When white mobs attacked blacks, Detroit police—many of whom were from the South—violently subdued blacks. Before federal troops were called in to end the city's "Bloody Week," 25 blacks and 9 whites had been killed, 319 people were injured, and 1,500 were arrested.

When the draft was introduced, over one million blacks were called up for military service. To their dismay, they found that the Army was still segregated. One black private asked bitterly, "Why are we expected to fight racism in Europe, but not in our own country?"

In 1942 a threatened lawsuit by the NAACP forced the

Army to accept a few black pilots. But as black fighter pilot Louis Purnell recalled, "We always had to be twice as good" to win promotion or be deployed in action.

Two years later the first integrated Army unit of the twentieth century was formed when twenty-five hundred black GIs joined a white combat unit. In July 1948, Walter White of the NAACP pressured President Harry S. Truman into ordering "equality of treatment of all persons in the Armed Services without regard to race, color, religion, or national origin." But segregationists sabotaged his order, and the armed forces were not fully integrated until 1950 when the United States entered the Korean War.

At the end of World War II, black veterans returned home to find the forces of segregation and violent racism still strong. And lynching was still a favorite tactic to put blacks "back in their place."

"Almost every victim of lynching since the war has been a veteran," observed John Gunther in his book *Inside U.S.A.* "The Negro community is . . . more aggressive in its demand for full citizenship—even in the South—than at any other time in history. . . . [Black soldiers] learned what their rights were; overseas, many were treated decently and democratically by whites for the first time in their lives; the consequent fermentations have been explosive."

At an Atlanta meeting in March 1946, the Ku Klux Klan announced that it was back in business. That year a mob of thirty Georgians murdered two black couples who had been driving in their car. In Louisiana, a mob kidnapped two young blacks, beat them savagely, then burned one to death with a blowtorch.

Local authorities made no arrests.

Some black heroes emerged in the 1940s. In 1944, Adam

Clayton Powell, Jr., became the first northern black to be elected to Congress. Representative John Rankin of Mississippi called his election a "disgrace" and vowed not to let Powell sit next to him. Mischievously, Powell made a point of persistently doing just that. One day he made the fuming Rankin move to a new seat five times.

Flamboyant behavior made Powell highly controversial, but white congressmen viewed him as a one-man civil rights movement. Immensely popular with his Harlem constituents, he was reelected to eleven consecutive terms, during which he moved up to powerful committee chairmanships.

Black sports fans and athletes were thrilled in 1947 when the Brooklyn Dodgers hired Jackie Robinson, the first black player to break the color ban in the major leagues. Robinson's success opened the door for other black athletes in professional sports.

In 1950 Ralph Bunche, who had mediated peace for the United Nations in the Arab-Israeli war two years earlier, became the first black to be honored with the Nobel Peace Prize. Orphaned at fourteen and once having worked as a janitor, Bunche's ascent to world fame made him an inspiration to blacks.

In the 1950s the NAACP made great strides in its fight against school segregation. Its strategy had been first developed in 1934 by black lawyer Charles Hamilton Huston. He declared, "The equal protection clause of the Fourteenth Amendment furnished the key to ending separate schools." Huston and his aide Thurgood Marshall would cite the Fourteenth Amendment and present to southern courts the documentation they had gathered on the inequality of southern black and white schools. They then demanded that southern communities upgrade black schools to equal those for whites, knowing that this would be so costly that the communities would have no choice but to integrate.

Their first major victory with this strategy was *Sweatt v. Painter*. The case involved a black mailman who applied to study law at the all-white University of Texas. Rather than admit him to the university, trustees opened a separate black law school for him. In 1950 the Supreme Court ruled that this was a violation of Sweatt's Fourteenth Amendment rights and for the first time ordered a black man to be admitted to an all-white institution.

The stage was now set for the Supreme Court's most sweeping ruling on education.

With the Supreme Court now liberalized under Chief Justice Earl Warren, the NAACP pleaded the case of *Brown v. Board of Education*. After listening to Thurgood Marshall's powerful arguments to overturn the decision that barred Linda Brown of Topeka, Kansas, from an all-white school, the court unanimously agreed to reverse the "separate but equal" concept that had been upheld ever since its 1896 ruling on *Plessy v. Ferguson*.

Chief Justice Warren declared in the historic ruling, "It is doubtful that any child may reasonably be expected to succeed in life if he is denied the opportunity of an education . . . available to all on equal terms. . . . To separate them from others of similar age and qualifications solely because of their race generates a feeling of inferiority . . . that may affect their hearts and minds in a way unlikely ever to be undone."

The court ordered all federal district courts to enforce public school integration in every state. In a later ruling, the court extended the ban on segregation to cover all tax-supported colleges and universities.

Hearing the news of the *Brown* decision, blacks were jubilant. One parade of celebrating blacks carried a coffin under the banner HERE LIES JIM CROW. The civil rights movement was now galvanized into action across America. Blacks put their lives on the line to turn the law into reality in the South. NAACP lawyers challenged segregation everywhere, and black organizations now began to press feverishly for the integration of all public facilities, as guaranteed by the Constitution and the Supreme Court.

White Citizens Councils in the South immediately organized to resist the court's decision. They claimed the right of "interposition"—interposing states' rights to block federal law when it threatened a state's local institutions. Mississippi Governor James Coleman urged every southern legislature to keep passing new state laws requiring segregation. "Any legislature can pass an act faster," he pointed out, "than the Supreme Court can erase it."

Where local courts ordered communities to integrate their schools by busing black students to white schools, angry white parents rioted to prevent the busing. White students chanted, "Two, four, six, eight, we don't wanna integrate!" Fewer whites were bused to black schools, which were often just tarpaper shacks.

To "keep the Nigra in his place," the White Citizens Councils used economic pressure, legal obstruction, intimidation, and arrests. The Ku Klux Klan used violence. Black schools and churches were bombed. White mobs in Mississippi committed the most racial violence, including three murders in 1955. Two were NAACP workers registering black voters. The third was fourteen-year-old Chicagoan Emmett Till, who was killed for "sassing" a white girl. For the first time, blacks across the nation broke their silence, demanding that Emmett's murderers be brought to justice.

White Mississippi jurors quickly acquitted the killers.

EIGHT

R O S A P A R K S sparked a national civil rights movement in 1955 by her arrest for refusing to give up a seat on a bus to a white man in Montgomery, Alabama. The incident led Reverend Martin Luther King, Jr., to organize a bus boycott in Montgomery that would last a full year.

After this first real desegregation victory, King and other black leaders organized the Southern Christian Leadership Conference (SCLC) in 1957. Dedicated to nonviolent civil disobedience, King and the SCLC would lead the national fight for black rights into the mid-sixties.

While the NAACP continued to win legal victories ensuring blacks equal access to education, enforcing those victories was another matter. When a federal court ordered the all-white University of Alabama to admit twenty-six-year-old Autherine Lucy, half the student body and the townspeople rioted in protest. The university's lawyers then suspended Lucy, arguing that she couldn't expect to overthrow overnight the prejudices of people held for three hundred years.

"The Emancipation Proclamation was ninety years ago," replied Thurgood Marshall. "I believe in gradualism. I think ninety years is pretty gradual." The court compelled Lucy's reinstatement, but the university trustees expelled her on concocted charges.

In defiance of another federal court order, Governor Orville Faubus of Arkansas ordered the National Guard to bar eight black children from entering Little Rock High School. A mob was allowed to riot and threaten the children with lynching, compelling the students' parents to keep them at home. Shown on national TV newscasts, these violent scenes shocked northern Americans and forced President Dwight Eisenhower to take action.

Reversing an earlier decision against the use of federal forces in state conflicts, Eisenhower sent Army troops into Little Rock to enforce integration. The black children returned to school behind federal bayonets. They had to be guarded from class to class by soldiers to protect them from the harrassment of white classmates who shoved and tripped them and spilled food trays over them.

Governor Faubus furiously protested, charging that Arkansas had been placed under military occupation and that the troops were "bludgeoning innocent bystanders, with bayonets in the back of white schoolgirls." After a year of "occupation," he stopped the integration of Arkansas's high schools by shutting them all down. He was easily elected to a third term as governor.

By 1960 black students had grown impatient with the slow progress toward integration. With the support of the SCLC, they formed the Student Nonviolent Coordinating Committee (SNCC). Together with black and white students in James Farmer's Congress of Racial Equality (CORE), they led a wide array of protests against segregation in all its forms throughout the South. Their ability to win national headlines made them the dynamic force behind change in the sixties.

SNCC and CORE organized a national boycott of retail chains that discriminated in the South. They staged sit-ins to integrate department store lunch counters. They mounted black voter registration drives. Through the Freedom Rides of 1961 they challenged the segregation of interstate buses and terminals.

Every protest of the young activists was met with furious resistance. While trying to register voters, they were thrown off southern plantations, beaten, whipped, gassed, and shot. In Montgomery, Freedom Riders' buses were attacked by a rioting mob, while the police—alerted in advance—remained conspicuously absent. In Birmingham, black men, women, and children were knocked down by powerful fire hoses, beaten with nightsticks, and bitten by police dogs. Throughout the South, tens of thousands were beaten and thrown into jail.

TV cameras captured it all for broadcast on the evening news. "I guess you could say we were partly responsible for the civil rights revolution," said a CBS-TV spokesman. "Certainly the conditions were already there, but no one knew it until fifty million Americans began seeing it on their screens." Seeing the growing sympathy of white northerners for southern blacks thanks to the news broadcasts, segregationists turned their anger against the newspeople. Newspeople were assaulted, their cameras smashed. In Oxford, Mississippi, two journalists were killed.

The deaths occurred in September 1962, during rioting over the admission of black James Meredith to the University of Mississippi. President John F. Kennedy had rushed sixteen thousand federal troops to the campus of "Ole Miss" to protect Meredith. The troops and the newsmen covering the story were shot at and attacked with bricks, rocks, and firebombs. The federal forces had to remain in Oxford for over a year to protect the university's one black student.

"Citizens are free to disagree with the laws of the United States," President Kennedy said, "not to disobey them."

By August 1963, when King organized his march on Washington, most Americans were firmly behind the struggle for civil rights. Two hundred thousand people attended the march, one of the largest demonstrations in American history.

Yet despite the growing support of white America, the violence did not abate. When Congress passed the Twenty-fifth Amendment in January 1964, SNCC and CORE organized the Mississippi Summer Project to register black voters. Segregationists responded by destroying almost forty black churches and beating up hundreds of activists. Three—two white, one black—were found murdered and buried under a dam.

Meanwhile, in the North, a Harlem riot erupted when a white off-duty police lieutenant shot a fifteen-year-old youth to death. The violence continued for several days, touching off other city riots.

By the mid-sixties, with the unceasing violence directed against nonviolent protesters in the South and the rising anger of poor blacks in northern ghettos, a new cry was being raised: "Black Power!"

N I N E

I N a final attempt to compel southern states to obey the spirit and letter of the Fourteenth Amendment, Congress passed the Civil Rights Act of 1964, which sharply defined and outlawed discrimination. The bill also established the Office of Economic Opportunity (OEO), which was endowed with a budget of almost $1 billion to be administered by local black leaders. The OEO was part of President Lyndon Johnson's "War on Poverty," a program designed to aid ghetto blacks and undercut the new Black Power movement.

Malcolm X, a member of the Nation of Islam, was the first nationally heard voice of Black Power. During Martin Luther King's nonviolent protest campaign in the South,

Malcolm X was urging the black community to unite in its own defense and to establish its own base of economic and political power. While King's support came mostly from the black middle class, Malcolm X's followers were poor urban blacks. Predicting a future with "more racial violence than Americans have ever witnessed," Malcolm X complained of leaders like King, "They're there just to restrain you and me, to restrain the struggle . . . not let it get out of control. Whereas you and I . . . want to smash everything that gets in our way."

In the summer of 1965, a major riot over alleged police brutality broke out in the black Watts ghetto of Los Angeles. It marked a sharp break with the nonviolent leadership of Martin Luther King. Lasting six days and involving 10,000 people, it left 34 dead, 875 injured, 4,000 arrested, and 209 buildings destroyed.

President Johnson tried to address the problems of the ghettos, where millions of black children lived in broken families on welfare. He launched Head Start, a program designed to help poor black preschoolers catch up with more advantaged children, and introduced the Child Nutrition Act, which provided free breakfasts to underprivileged children.

In the summer of 1966, even SNCC took up the cry for Black Power. Stokely Carmichael, the new leader of SNCC, explained the change: "Every cat's politics comes from what he sees when he gets up in the morning. The [white] liberals see Central Park, and we see sharecropping shacks." Adopting Marcus Garvey's slogan "Black Is Beautiful" and calling for blacks to take charge of their own lives, he became an international figure overnight.

White Americans' apprehension of the new movement and fear of more urban rioting was reflected by Congress's refusal to pass the 1966 Civil Rights Act—the first such set-back for the Johnson administration.

In 1966 blacks working within the system made important gains. For the first time in the history of Alabama, which now claimed hundreds of thousands of registered black voters, not a single candidate for governor that year uttered a word in defense of white supremacy. Massachusetts elected Edward Brooke to the Senate—the first black senator since Reconstruction.

The following year, Thurgood Marshall became the first black appointed to the Supreme Court. One month later in Cleveland, Carl B. Stokes became the first black mayor of a major northern city.

But for militant blacks these gains were too little, too late. Young radicals Huey Newton and Bobby Seale organized the Black Panther party in Oakland, California, demanding black control of the ghettos. With Minister of Information Eldridge Cleaver, they raised the slogan "Power to the People!" At rallies Panthers chanted, "The revolution has come—time to pick up the gun!"

Their followers rejected white culture, adopting Afro hairstyles, dashikis, and Black Power handshakes. To combat the police brutality that had plagued Oakland, they used their own cars to follow the police and monitor their activities, and stockpiled arsenals of weapons in their headquarters for self-defense. They won popular support by setting up their own community action program, serving free breakfasts to poor black children, setting up health care clinics, and providing child care for working mothers.

The Panthers rapidly grew to become a national organization, with chapters in thirty-three major cities, and their own newspaper, which the Panthers claimed had a circulation of two hundred thousand. As David Hilliard, who later became the Panthers' chief of staff, recalled, "We saw our struggle in terms not of being a revolutionary program, but simply to survive. We taught blacks *how*, not *what*, to think. . . . We also hoped white people would wonder why the Black Panthers could feed poor kids while the wealthy United States couldn't." But it was the Panthers' militant show of force, not the community programs, that drew the attention of white Americans.

In the summer of 1967, a new wave of urban riots struck the nation, the worst occurring in Newark, New Jersey, and Detroit, Michigan. In Detroit, over seventy-two hundred people were arrested and over forty were killed. The attitude of National Guardsmen dispatched to quell the riots was expressed by one soldier speaking to a reporter: "I'm gonna shoot me anything that moves and is black!"

The President's Advisory Commission was appointed to study the riots. Their findings were published in the Kerner Report, which placed the primary blame on police racism and repression. It also blamed the government's neglect of black needs for jobs, decent housing, and educational opportunities, as well as the media's poor coverage of the problems underlying race relations.

"Our nation is moving toward two societies," the report concluded, "one black, one white—separate and unequal."

A new Civil Rights Act was passed in 1968 aimed at gradually eliminating discrimination in housing and branding violations of civil rights as federal crimes. But southern congressmen succeeded in tacking on an anti-riot rider known as the Rap Brown Act, named after a Panther activist. This made it a federal offense to cross state lines "to further a riot."

The act had little effect on conditions in the ghettos, though the rider became a major tool in prosecuting black radicals.

The ghettos exploded again in April 1968 after the assassination of Martin Luther King. The death of the leader of nonviolent protest was met with rioting in over 125 cities, including Washington, D.C., where the violence almost reached the White House. Significantly, SNCC changed the word "Nonviolent" in its name to "National."

King's successor, the Reverend Ralph Abernathy, launched a Poor People's Campaign in the spring and summer of that year. A tent city was erected in Washington to dramatize the plight of the hungry and homeless. When demonstrators tried to stage a protest outside the Department of Agriculture, they were routed with tear gas.

The failure of the Poor People's Campaign was further demonstration of how the U.S. government had failed to address the problems of the poor and hungry. Funds earmarked for Johnson's War on Poverty were now diverted to pay for the escalating cost of the Vietnam War. In New York State, for example, welfare payments for a million families on relief, most of them black, were slashed to only 65 cents a day per person for food and clothing. This was generous compared to Florida and Texas, where the relief allotment was only 8 cents a day.

Mississippi had one of the worst records on hunger. Over a hundred thousand jobless black families there lost their sole source of food when the state switched from the free Surplus Commodity Program to the Food Stamp Program, which few could afford. Doctors investigating the problem for a January 1969 congressional hearing, found many black children so anemic and diseased that the children cried out in pain when the doctors merely moved their arms and legs. Many children, trying to live on tree bark, laundry starch, and clay, were dying of malnutrition.

By the end of the sixties, the militant cry for Black Power had been effectively silenced. Black militants' community programs had been overshadowed by ghetto violence. The Black Panthers, once the most visible Black Power organization, had ceased to exist as a national force.

When the Panthers first began monitoring the police for brutality, a grim feud broke out between them. Although police denied it, raids to seize weapons at Panther headquarters across the country seemed synchronized to wipe out the organization. In a two-year period police raided thirty-one Panther headquarters in eleven states, arresting over four hundred Panthers. The raids left nineteen Panthers and ten officers dead.

The raids climaxed at dawn on December 4, 1969. Fourteen Chicago policemen burst into the apartment where Panther leader Fred Hampton and seven party members were sleeping. Hampton was killed in his bed. While officers claimed they had fired only in self-defense, an investigation found that up to one hundred police bullets had been fired, with only one return shot.

Though ceasing to exist as a party, the Black Panthers did leave an important legacy. Their slogan of Black Power and rejection of white culture led to a new awareness of black culture and history, and the development of black studies in schools. In organizing blacks for community action they opened the way for many to enter the political system. As David Hilliard told me, "The Black Panthers were just a drop in the bucket, but we made a mighty big splash!"

T E N

A W H I T E backlash against ghetto turbulence and antiwar demonstrations in the fall of 1968 elected Richard M. Nixon president on a law-and-order campaign. Before his election, Nixon had promised southern leaders he would not enforce civil rights laws while in office. He kept his word when a northern furor arose over the issue of school busing.

In February 1970 a dozen southern Senators angrily demanded that the same federal guidelines used to integrate southern schools be applied to schools in the North. But attempts by the federal government to comply by launching a busing program met with a storm of opposition in northern cities.

Many middle-class whites had fled the cities for the suburbs in the sixties. The poorer whites left behind, fearing that integrated schools would lead to integration of their neighborhoods, furiously fought school busing. Black students from the ghettos were threatened and blocked from entering white schools. In September 1971, whites in Pontiac, Michigan, blew up the bus depot and set ten school buses on fire.

In 1972, Nixon won reelection by appealing to the alienated white "silent majority" and opposing school busing.

Most blacks, however, still favored integration. In the ghettos there was a growing belief that more black gains could be made by working with whites in the system than by burning the ghettos down. Many black politicians threw their hats into the electoral ring in the seventies. By 1973, such major cities as Los Angeles, Detroit, Atlanta, Washington, D.C., New Orleans, Newark, and Chicago had elected black mayors for the first time in their histories.

But the larger problems of civil rights violations and black poverty still remained. In November 1975, during the presidency of Gerald Ford, the U.S. Commission on Civil Rights reported that seven government agencies were refusing to enforce antidiscrimination laws.

"The black community," charged the NAACP in January 1976, "is being forced back into patterns that were commonplace during the Great Depression."

When Ronald Reagan was elected president in 1980, black Georgia legislator Julian Bond, who helped found SNCC, observed, "The government's attitude has changed from benign concern to malignant neglect." During the Reagan years, poor families received less government support than they had in 1947, and Bond noted that three million black children "had been shoved off the lunch line."

Shirley Chisholm had been elected in 1968 as the first black woman to sit in the House of Representatives, thanks to black support. In 1986, she expressed the discouragement felt by many over blacks' loss of fervor for civil rights: "Today we're like Rip Van Winkle, and we're fast asleep. . . . We sit paralyzed with our tongues plucked. We don't begin to move until our own front doorstep's attacked."

In 1984 the Reverend Jesse Jackson sought the Democratic nomination for president. Though he lost the nomination, his campaign was memorable for his call for a "Rainbow Coalition" of voters of every race to defeat Reagan's bid for a second term. In 1987 the Reverend Jesse Jackson formed Operation PUSH (People United to Save Humanity) to encourage black self-help. He induced black pride by getting ghetto youths to shout the mantra "I *am* somebody!" As a result of pressure on Congress by Jackson and other black leaders for affirmative action and equal opportunity programs, qualified blacks began getting some good jobs.

Jackson ran again for the Democratic presidential nomination in 1988. Increased black voter registration gave him a total of 3.2 million votes in Democratic primaries. But he lost the nomination to Massachusetts governor Michael Dukakis.

Dukakis lost in turn to George Bush, whose aides had run a racist campaign. Bush TV commercials tried to make Dukakis appear soft on black crime by featuring convicted black murderer Willie Horton, who on a work furlough from a Massachusetts prison had raped a white girl and stabbed her companion. It was a blunt appeal to white voters' fear of black criminals.

"The eighties gave people license to act upon their racial prejudices," said James Johnson, director of the Center for the Study of Urban Poverty at UCLA. He also charged that the two terms of the Reagan administration had declared "open season" on black Americans.

The economic boom of the Reagan years brought double-digit unemployment to the black community, leading to broken families riddled by poverty, and frustration for a generation of black men and women. The Bush administration that followed also ignored the plight of the black ghettos.

As the twentieth century wound to a close, America's thorniest problem remained, as it had been since the seventeenth century, racism.

(University of Chicago Library, Department of Special Collections)

Frederick Douglass

---

1 8 1 7 ? – 1 8 9 5

"Agitate! Agitate! Agitate!"

ONE

STANDING on the stable loft ladder fetching horse fodder, the sixteen-year-old Maryland slave felt a chill of terror as a callused hand suddenly seized his leg from below. Looking down, Frederick Douglass saw the scowling farmer intent upon roping his legs together. The beating this time, Frederick feared, would be the worst of all. He felt desperate.

Edward Covey had flogged him mercilessly for half the year Frederick had been hired out to the notorious "nigger-breaker." Covey's reputation in 1834 enabled him to hire cheap farmhands from slaveowners who wanted the spirits of their obstinate slaves broken. The scars on Frederick's back testified to Covey's brutal instruction.

But now Frederick felt he had reached the level of his endurance. Yet to resist was unthinkable. No slave dared try to stop a beating at white hands. The most he could do was try to huddle under the blows until his master or overseer grew exhausted or wearied of the sport.

Heart in his throat, Frederick sprang off the ladder. But Covey's grip on his leg brought him sprawling onto the stable floor with a crash. Covey sprang on him, attempting to tie his ankles. Frederick leapt away. Covey pounced on him again, fists cocked.

Frederick's last ounce of prudence vanished. Even if it meant his death for defiance, he would not take another beating. Each time Covey aimed a blow at his face, Frederick blocked it. Finally he gripped Covey's wrists so hard that his fingernails drew blood. Appalled by this unexpected audacity, Covey trembled with rage.

"Are you going to resist, you scoundrel?" he roared.

"Yes, sir," the young man replied politely through clenched teeth.

"Whence came the daring spirit . . . I do not know," he recalled later, adding, "The fighting madness had come upon me, and I found my strong fingers attached to the throat of my cowardly tormentor; as heedless of consequences, at the moment, as though we stood as equals before the law. The very color of the man was forgotten. I felt as supple as a cat, and was ready for the snakish creature at every turn. Every blow of his was parried, though I dealt no blows in return. I was strictly on the defensive, preventing him from injuring me, rather than trying to injure him. I flung him on the ground several times, when he meant to have hurled me there. I held him so firmly by the throat, that his blood followed my nails. He held me, and I held him." They struggled together for two hours.

Finally Covey bawled out to his cousin William Hughes to help him subdue the recalcitrant slave. Running to them, Hughes gripped Frederick's hands and tore them away from Covey.

"Got him!" Hughes exulted.

In one defiant motion Frederick swung his leg up savagely, kicking Hughes in the groin. Groaning in anguish, the cousin released his grip. He staggered back, bent over in pain, and lost any further interest in battle.

Aghast and totally taken aback, Covey looked from his moaning cousin to the audacious young slave on the floor.

"Do you mean to persist in your resistance?" he raged.

"I do, come what might!" Frederick panted. "You've used me like a brute for six months, and I don't intend to allow you to do it any more!"

Furious, Covey tried to drag him just outside the stable door toward a plank with which he could beat Frederick. But just as Covey leaned over to grab it, the young slave seized him by the collar with both hands and hurled him to the ground.

Suddenly frightened, Covey rose, panting. He stared at Frederick as though he had never seen him before. Grabbing him, Covey yelled for hired slave Bill Smith to help.

"What shall I do, Master Covey?" Smith asked innocently.

"Take hold of him, of course!" Covey howled.

Smith blinked his eyes. "Indeed, Master Covey, I just want to go to work."

"This *is* your work!" Covey roared. *"Take hold of him!"*

"My master hired me here to work, and not to help whip Frederick." Bill Smith walked off, leaving Covey speechless.

A huge, muscular young slave cook named Caroline came into the stable to milk the cows. Covey commanded her to come to his aid. She stared at Frederick, then shook her head.

"You *dare* refuse!" With one free hand Covey dealt her several blows. She stood her ground, then walked away.

Frederick felt a thrill of pride for the courage of Bill Smith and Caroline, proud of their bond to him of race. By now he was utterly exhausted by his struggle, but so was his white tormentor. Covey finally let him go.

"Now, you scoundrel, go to your work!" Covey puffed. "I would not have whipped you half as much as I have had you not resisted!"

"The fact was," Frederick wrote later, "he had not whipped me at all. He had not, in all the scuffle, drawn a single drop of blood from me. I had drawn blood from him; and even without this satisfaction, I should have been victorious, because my aim had not been to injure him, but to prevent his injuring me."

He added, "During the whole six months that I lived with Covey after this transaction, he never again laid the weight of his finger on me in anger. He would occasionally say he did not want to have to get hold of me again—a declaration which I had no difficulty in believing."

Frederick's experience convinced him that "men are whipped oftenest who are whipped easiest." The battle with Edward Covey was a turning point in his life as a slave.

"I was a changed being after that fight," he recalled. "I was *nothing* before; I was a *man* now, with a renewed determination to be a *free man*. I had reached the point at which I was *not afraid to die.* This spirit made me a free man in fact, though I still remained a slave."

TWO

M o s t histories credit only white abolitionists as the leaders of the fight against slavery. Actually, blacks who had been brought up in slavery were also in the vanguard of the abolitionist movement. And head and shoulders above these black Americans, physically and figuratively, stood Frederick Douglass.

Born into slavery in Talbot County on Maryland's eastern shore in 1817 or 1818, he was named Frederick Bailey. Even though his father was white, he was declared a slave because his mother was a slave. He never knew his father, who was suspected of being Thomas Auld, a slaveowner in the village of St. Michaels, to whom he was transferred at age nine. Seeing little of his mother, who died when he was only seven, Frederick was raised principally by his grandmother Betsey.

A handsome youngster, he frequently pondered the mystery of why a dark skin made him a slave, while those with white skin ruled as masters. The only answer he received to this question from Betsey was that God was good, and He knew what was best for everybody.

Frederick's first awareness of the cruelty suffered by slaves came at age six, when he was sent to live on the Lloyd Plantation owned by Captain Aaron Anthony. Although Anthony treated him with kindness, Frederick witnessed many instances of whipping inflicted upon the plantation's other slaves. When he was seven, his aunt and uncle fled north, and he dreamed for the first time of freedom.

At eight Frederick was sent to Baltimore to work at the home of Thomas Auld's brother, Hugh, and his wife. Sophia Auld was a kind, generous woman who favored Frederick enough to break the law by teaching him to read. Southern plantation owners frowned on making slaves literate, fearing they could then be agitated by northern abolitionist literature into revolting.

Frederick also taught himself to write, well enough even to forge "free passes" for slaves intent on running away. By blacking boots he earned a little pocket change, which enabled him to purchase a book called *The Columbian Orator*. Fascinated by reading its powerful speeches, he dreamed of becoming an orator so skilled he could persuade slaves of their right to freedom and whites of their obligation to grant it.

In Baltimore Frederick was allowed to mingle with white children, first as a playmate for Sophia's son, then in a Sabbath school. He told one of the students wistfully, "I wish I could be free, as you will be when you get to be a man. Have I not as good a right to be free as you?"

In 1833 he was returned to the home of Thomas Auld in St. Michaels. Here he was fed so stingily that he was forced to steal from Auld's larder. He did not consider it stealing but only taking food properly due him for his labor.

An older sister, Eliza, taught him slave techniques for safely frustrating masters. "Instead of disobeying," she advised, "play dumb." Masters considered slaves animals, so they weren't surprised when a slave acted like one. They were only irked, she explained, when slaves behaved like human beings.

A young white man named Wilson asked for Frederick's assistance in secretly teaching a Sabbath school. They assembled a dozen old spelling books and a few Bibles, with which they began teaching some twenty pupils to read. But on the second Sunday Thomas Auld learned of the school and led a white mob to attack it. Driving off the assembled blacks, they threatened dire punishment if the blacks there ever dared assemble again to be educated.

Exasperated by Frederick's participation, Auld decided to send him to the farm of Edward Covey to be "broken" of the bad habit of forgetting his place he picked up in Baltimore.

In 1835, after Frederick's bold defiance of Covey, he was reassigned as a field hand to a kindly farmer named William Freeland. Here he grew strong laboring at field work.

Although Freeland treated him relatively well, Frederick was still determined to run away to the North and freedom at the first chance. If a slave had a bad master like Thomas Auld or Covey, he reasoned, the slave yearned for a good master. And when the slave got a good master like Freeland, he yearned next to become his own master. One day, Frederick vowed, he would make that last wish come true.

THREE

W I T H that idea in the back of his mind, Frederick persuaded a free black man, James Mitchell, to allow another secret Sabbath school in his house. Frederick gathered some forty pupils, whom he taught to read three nights a week and Sundays. He soon discarded reading from the Bible, choosing instead selections about liberty and equality from his well-thumbed copy of *The Columbian Orator.*

Enlisting five other eager young slaves, Frederick organized a dangerous escape plan. He forged passes entitling each conspirator to visit Baltimore, their first waystation on the path to freedom. One of the group, however, grew nervous and betrayed the plans. Before the escapees could set on their journey north, four white constables on horseback seized them.

When one black youth, Henry Harris, was ordered to cross his hands to have his wrists bound, he refused. Two constables leveled pistols at him, threatening to blow him away.

"Shoot me, shoot me!" Henry flared. "You can't kill me but once. Shoot, shoot and be damned! I won't be tied!"

With courage inspired by Frederick's teaching about liberty and equality, Henry swept the pistols out of the constables' hands. All four lawmen fell on him, beating him mercilessly.

"Henry put me to shame," Frederick confessed later. "He fought, and fought bravely. . . . The fact is, I never saw much use of fighting where there was no reasonable probability of whipping anybody."

Bound together behind three strong horses, the captured barefoot slaves were dragged along a dusty road fifteen miles to jail. While imprisoned, they were subjected to poking and prodding by jeering slave traders and agents, who felt sure the

An illustration from *The Uncle Tom's Cabin Almanac* depicts
Frederick Douglass's flogging at the hands of Edward Covey. At
the age of sixteen, Douglass was sent to the infamous "slave-
breaker" as punishment for teaching other slaves to read.
(University of Chicago Library, Department of Special Collections)

rebellious slaves' masters would want to be rid of them. Frederick stolidly endured the humiliation of being handled like a horse.

The other slaves were finally released to their masters. A week later Thomas Auld reclaimed Frederick, warning him that many whites in the community were threatening to hang him as a ringleader. Auld decided that he had better send Frederick back to his brother, Hugh, in Baltimore to learn a trade.

In 1836 Hugh Auld placed Frederick with shipbuilder William Gardner, who employed seventy-five white and free black carpenters. The white workers, who hated the blacks, treated Frederick with contempt. "All niggers ought to be killed!" one snarled at him. Yet Frederick never forgot what he had learned from his struggle with the brutal Edward Covey. When any white workers struck him, Frederick struck back, regardless of consequences.

Once after a carpenter took a swing at him, Frederick lifted his attacker bodily and threw him in the water off the dock. Four white carpenters, enraged by his audacity, fell on him and beat him savagely. One booted him in the left eye, making his eyeball feel as though it had burst.

"Kill him! Kill him! Kill the damned nigger!" cried a white carpenter in a crowd of onlookers. "He struck a white man!"

The four assailants left Frederick sprawling in the dirt, covered with blood. Crawling to his feet, he picked up a spike and ran furiously after his attackers. But he was stopped and held by onlookers until his rage had subsided.

Knowing that Maryland law decreed thirty-nine lashes for any black who struck a white and that he was even more likely to be lynched by a white mob, he fled the shipyard and returned home.

Indignant on his behalf, Hugh Auld sought to have Frederick's four assailants arrested. But Maryland law prohibited any black from bringing evidence against a white. Frederick's scars of battle counted for nothing.

Auld placed him at another shipyard. Here Frederick became an expert caulker. Ironically, three of the ships he worked on were illegal slave ships, although it is uncertain that he knew this at the time.

Five of the new friends he made among the workers were free blacks. Frederick organized a secret debating club with them called the East Baltimore Improvement Society. At their meetings they argued over questions of slavery, freedom, and opportunities for blacks. Frederick told club members he had vowed to improve his fortunes until he was elected a U.S. senator.

During the years 1836 to 1838 the society also held social gatherings. At one social Frederick met a freeborn black woman named Anna Murray, who worked as a maid. Able neither to read nor write, Anna was fascinated by the erudite, proud, and audacious young slave. In 1838 they became engaged.

Meanwhile, Frederick's associations with free blacks made him resent more fiercely his own fate as a slave. He was by now a firm believer in abolition. He negotiated with Hugh Auld to buy his freedom by turning over half his wages every time he was paid. Auld allowed him to move into his own lodgings as a halfway step to freedom.

All went well until Frederick attended an out-of-town camp meeting with his friends, which made him a day late in paying Auld out of his wages. Auld was furious with him for daring to leave town without permission. Frederick was ordered to leave his shipyard job and move back under Auld's surveillance. Fearing that Auld might decide to sell him to someone in the Deep South, Frederick determined to risk a dash to freedom.

He hated the thought of leaving his friends and Anna, but planned to escape within three weeks. Meanwhile, to allay Auld's suspicions, he obtained work at another shipyard, turning over his full wages of $9 each week. Pleased, Auld gave him 25 cents and told him to "make good use of it." That he would, Frederick resolved silently. He would use it to help pay his fare on the Underground Railroad.

He promised Anna he would send for her from New York City. From a retired merchant sailor, Frederick managed to obtain a paper known as a "seaman's protection," certifying that the holder was a free American sailor. Then on Monday morning, September 3, 1838, he went to the railroad station dressed as a sailor. Waiting until a northbound train began to pull out, Frederick jumped aboard at the last minute.

When the conductor confronted him, asking for proof that he was a free black, he produced his spurious document. Frederick held his breath while the conductor examined it. After what seemed an eternity the conductor returned it, collected the fare to Wilmington, then continued up the aisle.

But Frederick still remained tense with anxiety. Delaware was also a slave state, filled with slavecatchers. As the train crawled on, Frederick recalled, "The heart of no fox or deer, with hungry hounds on his trail, in full chase, could have beaten more anxiously or noisily than did mine."

FOUR

FREDERICK worried that some free blacks on the train might recognize him and report him to the conductor. While his train stopped in a station, a southbound train pulled in on the opposite track. With a shock Frederick recognized a man who knew him well sitting at a window directly opposite him: the white captain of a revenue cutter he had worked on at a dockyard. He slid down in his seat in terror until the trains left the station.

A further shock was in store when a German blacksmith he knew entered his car and stared at Frederick intently. The blacksmith seemed puzzled by the seaman's outfit. "I really believe he knew me," Frederick wrote later, "but had no heart to betray me."

Leaving the train at Wilmington, he held his breath as he sought to board a steamboat for Philadelphia. Wilmington was well-known as a stalking ground for bounty hunters. Sometimes even free blacks were apprehended and taken south as slaves.

But finally he arrived in Philadelphia. "Free soil at last!" he marveled, hardly willing to believe his good luck. A black he asked directed him to the train for New York, which he reached after a twenty-four-hour journey to freedom.

His life in slavery was finally at an end. But he had not forgotten the millions of other slaves he had left behind to suffer the tortures of a miserable existence.

He sent for Anna, who, as a free black, was able to come at once. They were married by a minister whom Frederick could not pay, but who graciously accepted their thanks. How different, Frederick marveled, were the men of the wonderful North!

The Underground Railroad helped Frederick and Anna sail for Newport, Massachusetts. He was advised that at New Bedford he would be able to obtain work as a caulker in the shipyards where whaling vessels were outfitted.

Because blacks were not permitted in the cabin of even a

northern steamer, Frederick and Anna were compelled to spend a frigid fall night on deck. But after the hardships of Maryland, this seemed to them a minor inconvenience. Arriving at Newport wharf in the morning, they were observed looking uncertainly about by two black Quakers. One, Nathan Johnson, told them to get in the stage to New Bedford and paid their fare.

En route Johnson assured Frederick he need not fear recapture in New Bedford. However, he advised a change of name. Out of a copy of Walter Scott's *Lady of the Lake* he was reading, Johnson suggested the surname of Douglass. So Frederick Bailey began his life in the North as Frederick Douglass.

Five days later he went to the New Bedford wharves in search of work. On the way, observing a pile of coal in front of a minister's house, he asked the minister's wife for the job of bringing it in and putting it away. He left payment up to her. When he had finished she handed him two silver half-dollars.

"To understand the emotion which swelled my heart as I clasped this money," he wrote later, "realizing that I had no master who could take it from me—*that it was mine*—*that my hands were my own*, and could earn more of the precious coin—one must have been in some sense himself a slave."

He was stunned when he encountered his first instance of northern prejudice. Hired to work on a whaling vessel, he was instantly let go because all the white caulkers threatened to strike rather than work beside him. Frederick turned his hand to whatever menial job he could get—loading oil on a sloop, blowing bellows, sweeping chimneys, sawing wood, and waiting on tables. He averaged $1 a day. Anna worked as a maid.

They had four children, Rosetta in 1839, Lewis, Charles, and Annie.

Learning about William Lloyd Garrison's abolitionist paper *The Liberator,* Frederick subscribed to it. But he was impatient to hear a lecture in person. When he finally did, his brain reeled under the intellectual heresies of the firebrand abolitionist. Prejudice against color, Garrison thundered, was rebellion against God. The despised slaves were nearest and dearest to God's heart. Ministers who used the Bible to defend slavery served the devil, and their churches were synagogues of Satan. Americans who supported them, Garrison charged, constituted a nation of liars.

Garrison's fiery views inspired Frederick to dedicate his life to fighting the slavery he had escaped. He devoured every word of *The Liberator* each week. He never missed an abolitionist meeting of blacks in New Bedford. Hoping to emulate Garrison as an orator, he trained his voice to become, as it would later be called, "one of the great instruments of the nineteenth century."

At the age of twenty-one, standing over six feet tall, with a mass of wiry hair over broad, powerful features and an intense gaze, Frederick Douglass became a leading speaker at New Bedford's black church meetings.

When Garrison held a large convention of the American Anti-Slavery Society in Nantucket, Rhode Island, in the summer of 1841, Frederick managed to scrape up the fare to attend. He was surprised when a white abolitionist who had heard Frederick speak to blacks greeted him and invited him to address the meeting with a few words about his experiences as a slave.

Trembling at speaking to his first white audience, especially with Garrison present, Frederick stammered through some recollections of his enslavement. To his relief, his speech was applauded enthusiastically. And to his amazement, he saw Garrison weeping in pity at his disclosures. He was even more surprised when Garrison rose to speak and used Frederick's revelations as his text in a passionate plea for freeing the slaves.

After the meeting Frederick was thrilled when John A. Collins, general agent of the society, invited him to become a lecturer for the movement. An articulate fugitive slave, Collins explained, was just what they'd needed. Nothing would stir audiences like a black refugee from the South describing the brutality of slavery he'd endured.

Frederick hesitated. What if Thomas Auld heard about his lectures and sent a slavecatcher to retrieve him? But Garrison insisted, "You must tell these things to Northerners and shock them out of their complacency!" Frederick, flattered, let himself be persuaded to work for the society for three months.

One week later, at an abolitionist meeting at Millbury, he took part in the speeches along with Garrison and fellow abolitionist Wendell Phillips. His intelligence, his imposing physique, his dignity, and the rolling thunder of his eloquent voice made the white abolitionists rejoice that they had made no mistake in enlisting Frederick's services.

Speaking for the society, he felt for the first time the equal of white Americans. "For a time," he recalled, "I was made to forget that my skin was dark and my hair crisped."

F I V E

GARRISON viewed Frederick as a splendid example of the potential within every slave—an answer to slaveholders who insisted that blacks were unfit for freedom. For the next four years Frederick lectured brilliantly a hundred times a year from Nantucket to Indiana on the evils of slavery.

Introducing Frederick to audiences as "a piece of southern property," the meeting chairman would assure them that "it" could speak. Then the first fugitive slave lecturer would describe the things he had seen or experienced as a slave—young slave girls whipped for rejecting the advances of white masters, naked children sleeping on cold winter nights with their feet in warm ashes to keep from freezing, slave beds that were just horse blankets on shed floors, slaves wakened by whipping, overseers who flogged resting field-workers, and children fighting at pig troughs for enough food to ease the pangs of hunger.

In his travels across the country, Frederick constantly refused to give up his seat in cars segregated for white passengers. This was in keeping with Garrison's injunction to his followers to resist antiblack laws nonviolently, a technique that would later become the guiding principle of the civil rights movement led by Martin Luther King.

But while Frederick's resistance was peaceful, the response it received wasn't. Sometimes he was soundly beaten by the conductor and brakeman. Once a conductor called on six white passengers to throw him off the train. He clung so fiercely to his position that he tore out two seats.

The railroad superintendent was so infuriated that he ordered all trains not to stop in Lynn, Massachusetts, the Douglass's home since October 1841. Lynn's residents supported their neighbor and denounced the railroad for its bigotry.

After moving to Lynn, Frederick expanded his speeches to attack not only southern slavery, but northern prejudice as well. He was often heckled by bigots and proslavery rednecks who threatened to break up his meetings. But frequently his powerful voice was able to blast them into silence. His commanding presence usually made toughs hesitate to tangle with him. And when they did, Frederick's wit made fools of them.

When he attended an annual American Anti-Slavery Convention in New York City, toughs led by Tammany Hall political boss "Captain" Isaiah Rynders sought to break up the convention.

As Frederick was summoned to the rostrum to speak, Rynders jumped up and snarled, "If you speak disrespectfully of the South or any of our great Americans, I'll knock you off the stage!"

Frederick calmly held out his hands to the audience. "I offer myself to your examination. Am I a man?"

"Yes!" thundered the abolitionist audience.

"*You* are not a black man," Rynders jeered. "You are only half a nigger!"

Frederick bowed. "Then I am half-brother," he mocked, "to Captain Rynders."

The tabernacle rocked with laughter. Rynders glowered but made no further attempt to match wits with the black abolitionist. Next morning, however, backed by city hall, he and his toughs forced the convention to shut down.

At Richmond, Indiana, Frederick and abolitionist audiences were pelted with rotten eggs and brickbats. At Pendleton a mob of sixty southern-born roughnecks tore down the abolitionists' outdoor platform, and attacked the speakers with clubs. Frederick snatched away a club and sought to defend his colleagues, but it was wrested away from him.

"Kill the nigger!" roared an assailant. Frederick was severely beaten and knocked unconscious, his right hand broken. The experience, he related, "haunted my dreams," but failed to daunt him from speaking out in hostile territory.

Usually Frederick opened society meetings by relating his slave experiences. Garrison would follow with an analysis of slavery and an exhortation to fight against it. Gradually, however, Frederick began to inject his own comments into his talk.

This did not sit well with the white abolitionists, who urged him to stick to his stories of slavery and leave the thinking to Garrison and Phillips. One warned, "People won't believe that you were ever a slave, Frederick, if you keep on this way."

But he felt that he was growing intellectually and resented being used simply as an exhibit. The white abolitionists began to view him as cantankerous, too concerned about his own dignity. Some of them who preached racial equality, Frederick reflected wryly, were slow to practice it.

When Frederick spoke at Marlboro Chapel in Boston in August 1843, prejudice was still rooted even in the cradle of American liberty. Henry Bowditch, one of Garrison's earliest supporters, grew uneasy when Frederick accepted a dinner invitation Bowditch gave out of politeness.

"It is useless to deny," Bowditch confessed, "that I did not like the thought of walking with him in open midday up Washington Street. I *hoped* I would not meet any of my acquaintances."

And Bowditch was a staunch abolitionist.

Frederick's eloquence did raise increasing doubts among audiences that anyone so intelligent, gifted, and poised could really have been a slave. Some suggested that he was really an educated northern black being foisted on the public as an abolitionist hoax. Once a heckler challenged his authenticity.

Frederick removed his shirt and turned his back to the

audience. "The scars on my back," he roared, "are my authority for speaking from firsthand experience!"

To silence doubters once and for all, in 1845 Frederick wrote his autobiography, *Narrative of the Life of Frederick Douglass*. It had the same power and impact of *Uncle Tom's Cabin* published seven years later. He subsequently updated it in 1855, and again in 1881.

The book was so widely discussed that it put Frederick in danger of recapture by slavecatchers operating under the Fugitive Slave Law. In fact, in some cities mobs attacked him as an "escaped convict." Friends and supporters urged him to leave for England immediately to escape recapture.

S I X

In 1846 Frederick sailed for England on the Cunard line with white abolitionist friends. They were indignant when he was refused accommodation as a cabin passenger, but Frederick soothed them with assurances that he was used to being shunted off to steerage.

Despite this act of discrimination, the captain invited him to deliver a lecture on slavery to the ship's passengers. Several southerners aboard threatened to throw him overboard if he dared speak. But the captain rebuked them severely, cowing them into sullen silence.

Their threat to Frederick was reported in England when the southerners rushed to denounce him to the London press as a "worthless and insolent Negro." Their tactic backfired, and national interest was aroused by the black American visitor, who found himself welcomed warmly wherever he spoke.

"Whatever may be said of the aristocracies here," he mused later, "there is none based on the color of a man's skin.

This species of aristocracy belongs preeminently to 'the land of the free, and the home of the brave.' "

British abolitionists sent Frederick on a lecture tour through England, Ireland, and Scotland. They also raised $700 to buy his freedom from Hugh Auld, and another $2,500 to start a *black* abolitionist paper in the United States.

The purchase of his freedom stirred anger among some abolitionists, who charged that Frederick's compliance signified recognition of a slave as property to be bought and sold. Garrison defended the transaction as not a sale, but the payment of ransom.

After a successful eighteen-month tour abroad, Frederick toyed briefly with the idea of settling in England, which had abolished slavery in 1807. He decided against it, however, for fear that Anna and his "dark children could never be at home in this foreign country." But primarily it was his eagerness to publish a black antislavery paper of his own that led him to return to Boston in April 1847.

After a summer spent on a lecture tour with Garrison, Frederick revealed that he would be starting his own abolitionist newspaper. Garrison felt that his *Liberator* newspaper was enough for the cause and that Frederick would do more good on the lecture circuit. But on December 3, 1847, in Rochester, New York, Frederick edited and published the first issue of *The North Star*. For the white abolitionists it proclaimed, *"He who has endured the cruel pangs of Slavery* is the man to advocate liberty. It is evident we must be our own representatives and advocates . . . in connection with our white friends."

Garrison was furious. He wrote his wife, "Such conduct grieves my heart. His conduct about the paper has been impulsive, inconsiderate, and inconsistent."

Douglass's eighteen-month-long lecture tour of Britain was a resounding success. Although originally traveling to England to escape recapture under the Fugitive Slave Law, he soon began appearing at meetings such as the above, where thousands gathered to hear him speak. *(University of Chicago Library, Department of Special Collections)*

The establishment of *The North Star* marked a new direction for Frederick. He no longer saw himself as just an exhibit of white abolitionists standing before white audiences. Now he was a leading spokesman for his race, a black editor addressing a principally black leadership. Indeed, soon blacks began calling him the Great Frederick, personification of their hopes for citizenship and racial justice.

Frederick published *The North Star* for thirteen years in the first print shop ever owned by an American black, a fact of which he was proud. As an editor he dealt not only with southern slavery, but with the bigotry and injustice against northern blacks. Yet Frederick did not blame only white Americans for the miserable lives suffered by most blacks. "It is evident that we can be improved and elevated," he told his readers, "only just so fast and far as we shall improve and elevate ourselves."

In Frederick's thinking, if *he* could rise to his position in life from his own lowly slave origins, then *any* determined black could surely follow his example.

Although he presented an exemplary public figure, in private his character was not without flaws. "He rejoiced," one reporter quoted him, "to be like white folks." He could not help critically contrasting his stout, plain, dark-skinned wife Anna with many of his white female admirers. And according to rumor, he had affairs with several of them.

He unquestionably enjoyed the company of middle- or upper-class white women. In 1848 he attended the Women's Rights Convention in Seneca Falls, New York, the only male present who made a speech strongly endorsing the resolution demanding women's suffrage.

The North Star was the only paper that consistently carried news of the women's movement. He gave the first

National Women's Rights Convention in 1850 its slogan, "Equality before the law, without distinction of sex or color." He attended almost all feminist meetings in that decade as a principal speaker.

"When I ran away from slavery, it was for myself," he said later. "When I advocated emancipation, it was for my people. But when I stood up for the rights of women, self was out of the question, and I found a little nobility in the act."

While editing *The North Star*, Frederick did not abandon his abolitionist lectures. In June 1849 he shocked a white audience in Boston by telling them, "I should welcome the intelligence tomorrow, should it come, that slaves had risen in the South, and that the sable [black] arms which had been engaged in beautifying and adorning the South were engaged in spreading death and devastation." As the audience gasped, he calmly reminded them that Americans had cheered the bloody French Revolution against royalist oppressors. So why shouldn't they hail a similar bloody revolution by southern slaves?

S E V E N

WHEN Congress passed the new Fugitive Slave Act of 1850, making it illegal to interfere with the arrest of a fugitive slave, northerners took action. Rather than cooperate with southern slaveholders, many began obstructing enforcement of the act. Abolitionists clashed bloodily with bounty hunters who kidnapped free northern blacks in place of slaves they could not catch.

In turn, abolitionists suspected of being in the Underground Railroad were threatened with violence, house burnings, and murder. Nevertheless, Frederick continually raised money to assist escaped slaves and contributed fees from many of his lectures to help them.

Frederick also took an active role in helping fugitive slaves, serving as "stationmaster" of the Rochester terminus of the Underground Railroad. Over the course of ten years, he helped four hundred slaves flee to freedom. As dangerous as his own actions were, Frederick hailed escaped slave Harriet Tubman as "the Moses of her people." An illiterate field hand, Harriet risked her freedom and her life in nineteen perilous trips south to help free over three hundred slaves. Frederick wrote her, "Most that I have done has been in public, and I have received much encouragement. . . . You on the other hand have labored in a private way. . . . The midnight sky and the silent stars have been the witnesses of your devotion to freedom and of your heroism."

While working to help slaves escape from the South, Frederick still had to fight northern prejudice. It troubled him deeply when his children were faced with discrimination.

"My children were not allowed in the public school in the district in which I lived, owned property, and paid taxes," he complained, "but were compelled to go over to the other side of the city to an inferior colored school. I sought and obtained a hearing before the Board of Education, and after repeated efforts with voice and pen, the doors of the public school were opened . . . [to] colored children."

Frederick's espousal of political action as the way to win freedom and justice for blacks further deepened the rift between him and William Lloyd Garrison. Garrison opposed seeking legislation as futile. The only hope, he was convinced, lay in northerners cutting free of the South. "The sooner the Union goes to pieces," he told the American Anti-Slavery Society grimly, "the better!"

On May 9, 1851, Frederick made the break between himself and Garrison open, and the two became bitter enemies. From that point on Frederick led the black abolitionist movement separately from Garrison's white crusaders. In *The North Star* he urged blacks to become politically active, pursuing "assimilation through self-assertion." At times he seemed to advocate violence to achieve black aims, but at other times, peaceful measures.

Frederick published his second autobiography in 1853. *My Bondage and My Freedom* included his experiences abroad and also talked about his grandmother, half-sisters, and half-brothers.

That same year, Frederick visited Harriet Beecher Stowe, author of the powerful novel about the cruelties of slavery, *Uncle Tom's Cabin*, published in 1852. Mrs. Stowe admired Frederick greatly and wished to discuss establishing a school for black youths. The plan failed to materialize, but she turned over $535 she had raised for Frederick's personal use.

"As a colored man he has peculiar disabilities," she explained, "and we thought it no more than right that he should have peculiar encouragements."

E I G H T

A N E W Supreme Court decision in March 1857 had a tremendous impact on race relations, setting the stage for the Civil War. *Dred Scott v. Sandford* involved a Missouri doctor who had spent four years in Illinois and what is now Minnesota, taking with him his slave, Dred Scott. Missouri was a slave state, but the others were not. In 1847, following their return to Missouri, Dred Scott sued for his freedom in the state courts. When he lost, an abolitionist congressman pressed the case up to the Supreme Court.

Chief Justice Roger B. Taney rendered the majority decision that slaves were not citizens and therefore could not sue in federal courts. A slave from a slave state was not made free by residence in free territory. And the Fifth Amendment prohibited depriving persons of their property without due process.

"At the time of the Declaration of Independence . . . and for more than a century before," wrote Justice Taney, "they [slaves] had been regarded as being . . . so far inferior that they had no rights which the white man was bound to respect."

This decision led a bitter Garrison to brand the Constitution a "pro-slavery document." Frederick was also shocked by it, but refused to let it shake his determination to end slavery through legislation and reform.

In 1847 Frederick first met white-bearded abolitionist Captain John Brown, who, like Garrison, believed that political activists would never be able to abolish slavery.

"These men are all talk," he sneered to Frederick. "What is needed is action, *action!*" Brown wanted to instigate a slave insurrection in Virginia, but Frederick was dubious that such a rash plan could succeed. Still, Brown's passionate conviction made him wonder if he was wrong in hoping to abolish slavery peacefully. They met and corresponded often over the next two years. Then in late September 1859, Brown asked Frederick to meet him, bringing what money he could spare.

When they met near Chambersburg, Pennsylvania, Brown revealed his plan to raid the town of Harper's Ferry, Virginia, seize the arsenal, arm fifteen hundred local slaves, then lead them south, freeing slaves along the Appalachians and establishing a free black state.

Frederick pleaded with Brown not to execute his plan, as it would constitute an attack on the federal government, which would send the Army to surround him and force his surrender. If that happened, Brown replied, he would take local citizens hostage to win his way out of any blockade.

"Virginia would blow you and your hostages sky-high," Frederick warned, "rather than let you hold Harper's Ferry an hour!" But Brown was obstinate and even urged Frederick to join him.

"My discretion or my cowardice," Frederick recalled, "made me proof against the dear old man's eloquence—perhaps it was something of both."

On October 16, 1859, Brown led fourteen white men and five blacks in the attack on Harper's Ferry. Seizing the federal arsenal and armory, they took sixty leading citizens hostage. To Brown's chagrin, no slaves dared join him. After two days of fierce fighting with U.S. Marines led by Colonel Robert E. Lee, Brown and his surviving followers were taken prisoner.

Brown's carpetbag was found to contain letters and documents implicating Frederick and other abolitionists. Frederick's friends urged him to flee at once to escape charges of conspiracy. "I knew that all Virginia," he recalled later, "were I once again in her clutches, would say, 'Let him be hanged.' "

Frederick fled to Quebec, and from there on November 12 took passage again for England. He gloomily felt that he was being forced into exile, perhaps for life. But after six months abroad, he received word that his eleven-year-old daughter Annie had died, and he resolved to return home secretly.

By the time he arrived, the execution of Brown and his raiders had satisfied the thirst of Virginians for revenge. Besides, fiery denunciations of their state throughout the North for its lynch-style justice had made them anxious to put the

William Lloyd Garrison, LEFT, Harriet Tubman, RIGHT, and John Brown, BELOW CENTER. Their tactics were different but their goal was the same: freedom for all slaves. *(University of Chicago Library, Department of Special Collections)*

whole affair behind them. So when Frederick surfaced publicly, no attempt was made to extradite him.

Twenty-two years later, in an address delivered at a Harper's Ferry college, Frederick said, "John Brown began the war that ended slavery and made this a free republic. Until this blow was struck, the prospect for freedom was dim, shadowy and uncertain."

When Abraham Lincoln ran for president in 1860 against slavery advocates Stephen Douglas and John Breckinridge, Frederick threw himself into the campaign for Lincoln. Despite the racist views Lincoln had expressed in previous campaigns, Frederick now pinned his hopes on the man who told Americans, "this government cannot endure permanently half *slave* and half *free*."

But after Lincoln was elected, Frederick was vexed at his hesitation to free the slaves. In 1860 Lincoln accepted a plan by the American Colonization Society asking Congress for a $600,000 appropriation to buy the freedom of several hundred slaves, who were then deported to an island near Haiti. Many died of disease; the rest had to be repatriated.

Frederick was incensed at this concept of "freedom" for American slaves. He declared himself "bewildered by the spectacle of moral blindness, infatuation and helpless imbecility which the government of Lincoln presents."

N I N E

W H E N the Civil War broke out on April 12, 1861, Frederick was even more incredulous when Lincoln canceled a decree by General John Fremont freeing all slaves whose masters were fighting against the North. Lincoln also ordered that no blacks were to be armed, because to do so would create a dangerous and fatal controversy in Union ranks, "doing more harm than good."

If he were to use black troops, Lincoln told clergymen, he feared that "fifty thousand bayonets in the Union army from the border states" would go over to the Confederates. Frederick challenged this view. He reproached Lincoln for letting the North fight "with their soft white hand, while they kept their black iron hand chained and helpless behind them."

Lincoln was finally won over by the argument that fifty thousand armed and well-drilled black soldiers upon the banks of the Mississippi might frighten the rebels into instant surrender.

When Lincoln reluctantly ordered the raising of black troops, Frederick enthusiastically set about recruiting two black regiments. Enlisting his own sons, Charles and Lewis, he raised black hopes that the war would liberate all slaves. Lincoln, however, made no such promise, despite Frederick's urging.

Even now Lincoln clung to his belief that the best solution to the black problem in America was to encourage the emigration of all blacks to Central America in a colonization scheme. On August 14, 1862, he summoned a group of black leaders to the White House to urge them to support this plan.

"You and we are different races," he told them. "We have between us a broader difference than exists between any other two races. Whether it is right or wrong I need not discuss, but this physical difference is a great disadvantage to us both. . . . Even when you cease to be slaves, you are yet far removed from being placed on an equality with the white race. . . . Go where you are treated the best. . . . Latin Americans are more generous than we are. To your colored race they have no objections."

Lincoln also suggested that the "mere presence" of blacks had caused the war. Now Frederick was thoroughly outraged. He accused the president of being "a genuine representative of American prejudice and Negro hatred."

On January 1, 1863, Lincoln finally gave in to the abolitionists' pressure and reluctantly signed the Emancipation Proclamation freeing the slaves in the Confederacy.

"I claim not to have controlled events," Lincoln admitted ruefully, "but confess plainly that events have controlled me."

Although it had taken Lincoln two years in office to reach this decision, Frederick was jubilant and entirely willing to forgive him. "In that happy hour," he recalled, "we forgot all delay . . . all tardiness."

The proclamation inspired black celebrations throughout the North, with Frederick in great demand as the most important and most exciting black speaker. That January he traveled over two thousand miles and was hailed everywhere by thousands of blacks. The celebrations, Frederick exulted, were very much in order—"a day for poetry and song." No one noted that the proclamation still had not freed slaves in the North or Midwest. It was generally assumed that event would follow victory.

But Frederick grew indignant once more when he learned of discrimination in the Union forces. In July he went to Washington to complain to the president. Lincoln's cordial reception of him flattered Frederick and won him over.

"I was an ex-slave, identified with a despised race," he wrote later, "and yet I was to meet the most exalted person in this great republic. . . . He bade me welcome. I at once felt myself in the presence of an honest man—one whom I could love, honor, and trust without reserve or doubt."

Frederick told Lincoln that he could not continue recruiting blacks for the Union forces, however, because they were not being paid the same as whites. When taken prisoner, they received much harsher treatment than whites. Nor were they rewarded with medals and promotions for bravery like white troops.

Lincoln evaded these issues, but promised Frederick to give field commissions to any black troops recommended by the secretary of war. Frederick came away from the meeting a changed man, still disagreeing with the president, but completely convinced of Lincoln's sincerity and belief in equality.

"I found him entirely free from popular prejudice against the colored people," he reported now. "He was the first great man that I talked with in the United States freely, who in no single instance, reminded me of the difference between himself and myself, of the differences of color."

That bespoke Lincoln's skill at personal relations, as well as Frederick's susceptibility to flattery from the White House. Only a year earlier the black delegation Lincoln had received at the White House had considered him an extreme racist.

Next month Frederick ceased publication of *The North Star*, which had been renamed first *Frederick Douglass' Paper*, then *Douglass' Monthly*, ending his fifteen years as an influential editor.

During another visit to the White House, Frederick learned that the president was disturbed because the Emancipation Proclamation had not led southern slaves to bolt for northern lines as quickly and as numerously as he had hoped.

"Slaveholders know how to keep such things from their slaves," Frederick suggested, "and probably very few know of your Proclamation."

"Well, I want you to set about devising some means of making them acquainted with it, and bring them into our lines," the president replied.

Frederick promptly set about organizing a band of black scouts to penetrate southern lines to carry the news of emancipation and to urge the slaves to escape north to freedom.

Frederick was next summoned to the White House for advice on Lincoln's reelection campaign. By now he considered the president's remaining in office the best hope of destroying slavery entirely. Working hard for Lincoln's reelection, he was rewarded by becoming the nation's first black invited to attend an inaugural White House reception. But when he sought to enter the executive mansion, two policemen blocked his way, telling him that no persons of color could be admitted.

Indignant, Frederick sent an appeal to the president. Lincoln instantly summoned him, declaring, "Here comes my friend Douglass." Taking Frederick by the hand, he said, "I am glad to see you. I saw you in the crowd today, listening to my inaugural address. How did you like it?"

"Mr. Lincoln, that was a sacred effort!"

"I am glad *you* liked it."

The two policemen's jaws dropped in disbelief and chagrin.

TEN

LINCOLN'S respect for black troops increased considerably when they won praise from General Ulysses S. Grant for their gallantry in battle. "At some times," Lincoln said with a smile, "it was just as well to be a little color-blind."

Changing his mind about the advisability of exiling blacks to Central America, he told a white audience that since blacks

"Contraband" working for the Union Army, 1864. During the
Civil War, southern blacks who made their way behind Union
lines were known as "contraband." No longer slaves, they passed
on much information about Confederate troop movements.
(University of Chicago Library, Department of Special Collections)

had staked their lives for the Union, American whites must keep their promise to award them freedom.

As the war wound to a close, however, Frederick doubted that Lincoln intended to make freed southern slaves citizens by giving them the vote. There were indications that the president felt white southerners would never stand for sharing the ballot booth with their former slaves.

When the war ended on April 9, 1865, Lincoln admitted at Petersburg, Virginia, "I have been only an instrument. The logic and moral power of Garrison, and the antislavery people of the country, and the army, have done all."

Frederick was stunned five days later by news of Lincoln's assassination. Mourning the loss, he was deeply touched when Mrs. Lincoln sent her husband's walking stick to him. Lincoln had asked her to present Frederick with a token of his regard.

Ratification of the Thirteenth Amendment abolished all slavery. But Frederick knew that southern slaves would need enormous help to survive freedom. What little security they had had, wretched as it had been, was now stripped away, and they would have to fend for themselves.

Frederick was doubtful that they could expect any help from the new president, Andrew Johnson, a Democrat who had been elected with Republican Lincoln on a national unity ticket. He pressed Johnson and the Congress for an agency to protect freedmen's rights and to settle them on confiscated Confederate lands. Congress responded with an act setting up a Freedman's Bureau, primarily hoping to keep freed slaves from moving north.

Meanwhile, Frederick drew large crowds to a lecture tour he made crusading for black suffrage. In February 1866 he was appointed to a black committee to pursue this demand with the president. When the delegation met with the president, Johnson told Frederick that the right to vote was subject to state laws and that forcing the franchise for blacks on southern whites would precipitate a race riot.

"On the contrary, Mr. President," Frederick replied coldly, "enfranchisement of the colored man will prevent, rather than stimulate, a race riot."

"The problem would best be solved," Johnson snapped, "by emigration." Privately the president feared that politically active southern blacks would sharply reduce white power.

Frederick turned to the delegation and growled, "The president sends us to the people, and we go to the people."

He pressed Congress to muster opposition to Johnson's policies. Congress responded by overriding the president's veto of the Freedmen's Bureau Act in April and defiantly enacting a second Freedmen's Bureau Act three months later.

Frederick himself would later be offered the post of commissioner at the Freedmen's Bureau by President Johnson. While Frederick aspired to high office, he knew the offer was politically motivated and he declined. He did not, he explained to his followers, want to "place myself under any obligation to keep the peace with Andrew Johnson." A white friend, editor Theodore Tilton, reported, "The greatest black man in the nation did not consent to become the tool of the meanest white."

When the American Anti-Slavery Society met in May 1866, Garrison proposed that the society now dissolve as unnecessary since the Thirteenth Amendment was in place. But Frederick objected strenuously during a two-day debate. Blacks had not yet been given absolute civil equality or the vote, he pointed out, and their new liberties in the South would need both vigilant enforcement and protection.

The membership supported Frederick's views. Garrison, shocked and hurt that his one-time protégé had caused repudiation of his leadership, angrily resigned from the society.

In his crusade for the black vote, Frederick joined forces with Susan B. Anthony, leader of the suffragettes. But she subsequently resented black competition for the ballot and refused to support the Fifteenth Amendment because it proposed enfranchising only blacks and not women. Frederick was incensed when Anthony made the mistake of suggesting that women deserved the vote first because they were "more intelligent" than black men.

Frederick lashed back that he was not demeaning woman suffrage just because he preferred the claim of blacks. Unlike women, he pointed out grimly, blacks were being "mobbed, beaten, shot, stabbed, hanged, burnt." The feminist and black crusades for the vote parted ways.

Between 1865 and 1875 Congress passed major civil rights legislation enforced by federal troops stationed in the South. "We have a future," Frederick now declared jubilantly. "Everything is possible to us." He threw himself enthusiastically into the crusade for the Fifteenth Amendment and was ecstatic when it was passed and ratified. But his optimism was premature.

Although blacks now had the legal right to vote, southern whites were grimly determined to see that they didn't use it.

ELEVEN

DURING the Reconstruction period following the Civil War, blacks faced countless obstacles in trying to vote. When registering, they might have to take a "literacy test" designed to fail blacks and pass whites. One educated black in Mississippi was asked to read a convoluted passage from the state constitution and explain what it meant. "It means," he replied gravely, "that no Negro can vote in Mississippi."

The Ku Klux Klan also helped southern whites steal elections. In 1868 a congressional investigation found that in the three weeks prior to election day in Louisiana, two thousand blacks had been murdered, wounded, or flogged. The message to blacks to keep away from the election polls was loud and clear.

The impact on white children as well as black in the South was appalling. One small white boy brought home from a lynching told his mother, "I've seen a man hanged; now I wish I could see one burned."

In the presidential race of 1868, Frederick campaigned strenuously for Republican Ulysses S. Grant, securing a large majority of black votes for the man he considered an unprejudiced friend of the black race.

When President Grant used military force to put down Klan violence in the South, Frederick praised him in his new newspaper, *The New National Era.* "I see in him," he told readers, "the vigilant, firm, impartial, and wise protector of my race from all the malign, reactionary, social, and political elements that would overwhelm them in destruction."

Frederick himself was nominated for vice president in 1872 on the ticket of the Equal Rights party, headed by controversial feminist Victoria Woodhull. He campaigned instead for Grant's reelection. When his Rochester home was destroyed by fire, he suspected arson by Democratic hirelings. He moved his family to Washington.

Frederick's persistent agitation helped bring about the first Civil Rights Bill in 1875. It required equal treatment for blacks in public conveyances, inns, and theaters. But in the segregated South this act quickly became a dead-letter law.

One black student at a college where Frederick spoke asked him afterward what advice he had for a young black man starting out in life. Frederick replied, "Agitate! Agitate! Agitate!"

Frederick continued to bring out the black vote for presidential candidates. When Rutherford B. Hayes declared that he would not interfere in southern affairs as long as the South obeyed laws respecting black rights, Frederick supported him in 1876.

In 1877 Hayes appointed Frederick U.S. marshal for the District of Columbia, the highest office ever held by a black up to that time. Barely in office a month, Frederick stirred a commotion with a Baltimore speech charging that Washington represented "a most disgraceful and scandalous contradiction to the march of civilization as compared with many other parts of the country."

Outraged cries arose for Frederick's removal from office, but Hayes stood by him. *The New York Times* observed that he had spoken the truth, told "never before by a man whose skin was dark colored, and . . . appointed to office in the District."

In June Frederick returned to St. Michaels in Maryland for a nostalgic visit, after a forty-one-year absence. He visited his former master Thomas Auld, who was now sick and dying. Auld shed tears at the sight of his one-time slave, now grown important and powerful. Frederick's voice choked with emotion.

So much had happened since they had last seen each other.

TWELVE

FREDERICK was appalled in 1883 when the Supreme Court, ruling in *United States v. Harris,* asserted that neither the Fourteenth nor Fifteenth Amendments were designed to deprive states of their control over elections. White northerners shrugged at the South's continued thwarting of black voting rights, Frederick believed, because many doubted blacks' qualifications to vote wisely.

"To the white people," he wrote in April 1883, "I say, Measure not the colored man from the heights you have attained, but rather the depths from which he has come—those depths into which you plunged him and held him for two centuries."

In the 1880s, Frederick served in political positions never attained by a black man before. President James Garfield made him recorder of deeds for the District of Columbia. He held the position until the following president, Grover Cleveland, asked him to resign so that Cleveland could award the post to another black as a political obligation.

When Frederick turned out the black vote for Benjamin Harrison in 1888, he was appointed minister-resident and consul general to Haiti. Harrison also appointed him chargé d'affaires for Santo Domingo. By now Frederick cut an impressive figure as an elder diplomat. The president of Haiti praised him as a shining example of "the moral and intellectual development of the men of the African race by personal effort and mental culture."

The U.S. government sought to win a lease for a naval base on Haiti, which the Haitians were extremely reluctant to grant. When they remained obdurate, American business interests involved in the lease accused Frederick's color iden-

Frederick Douglass serving as a marshal at the inauguration of
President James Garfield in 1881. The illustration is from
Douglass's last autobiography, *The Life and Times of Frederick
Douglass*. *(University of Chicago Library, Department of Special
Collections)*

tity with the Haitians of preventing him from making a genuine effort to obtain the lease. Disgusted, ailing at age seventy from the Haitian climate, Frederick submitted his resignation.

That proved his last public American office. He continued to lecture, became president of a black bank, and wrote a third updated autobiography. In his latter years, after the death of Garrison, he became reconciled with other leaders of the old American Anti-Slavery Society. They now recognized Frederick's great contributions to abolition and civil rights.

He, too, mellowed considerably in his last years' memories of Garrison. "I have often been asked where I got my education," he said. "I have arrived from Massachusetts Abolition University: Mr. Garrison, President."

Many honors now came his way. The citizens of Rochester, New York, commissioned a bust of Frederick for the University of Rochester, with an unveiling ceremony by the mayor. One university conferred upon the black ex-slave who had never gone to any school a doctor of laws degree. Another invited him to deliver a commencement address, which became his last powerful speech against Southern lynch law. In 1893 Haiti appointed him its commissioner at the first World's Fair in Chicago.

On February 20, 1895, he was invited to address a meeting of the Women's Council. He was escorted to the speaker's platform by no less a dignitary than Susan B. Anthony, with whom he was by this time also reconciled. All the women in the hall rose to their feet and waved their handkerchiefs in tribute to the first man who had championed their cause.

That night, describing this event to his second wife, Helen, he suddenly dropped to his knees and lost consciousness. A few minutes later, at the age of seventy-eight, Frederick Douglass was dead.

News of his death flashed throughout the United States. The legislatures of four northern states adopted resolutions of sorrow. Even the North Carolina legislature adjourned for the day out of respect for his memory.

When he lay in state at Rochester's City Hall, thousands filed past to take their last look at the former slave who had become a heroic symbol of freedom for his race.

THIRTEEN

FREDERICK Douglass was not without his critics. Some held that vanity had led him to believe his exceptional ability and public service placed him far above ordinary blacks. His message was flawed, others charged, because he believed that any black should be able to follow his success, "could be his own Moses" and lead himself out of the wilderness of poverty and prejudice. He was also criticized for seeking white social acceptance by consorting with white women and marrying one as his second wife.

Once Frederick had accepted an invitation to play croquet at the elegant mansion of a Washington socialite who employed his son-in-law as a stableman. As his own fortunes increased, some said, he lost the vision and compassion that had once endeared him to the black community as the Great Frederick.

He was also accused of placing political expedience and his own ambitions above recognizing the Reconstruction problems faced by blacks. It was true that he had let himself be used by presidents to win support from American blacks. But at the same time he had also used those presidents to win support *for* blacks, both slave and free.

Despite his human flaws, Frederick Douglass had been the one voice that had challenged the conscience of white

Americans by thundering out against prewar slavery and post-war lynchings. He had also exposed the hypocrisy of the North, which was persisting in prejudice while deploring southern racism.

And it could never be forgotten that he had won over millions of white Americans to the cause of emancipation by his eloquent, brilliant oratory during his lifelong fight for the civil rights of black Americans.

In 1903 Theodore Roosevelt, then governor of New York, unveiled a monument in honor of Frederick Douglass at Rochester. Sixty-one years later, in belated recognition of his greatness, Frederick's home in Anacosta Heights in the nation's capital was declared a national monument.

And in 1991 a new opera, *Frederick Douglass*, celebrating his life, was presented by the New Jersey State Opera. The librettist, Donald Dorr, said, "Frederick Douglass was an American hero. He overcame a great deal of prejudice and many obstacles in his path. . . . [He was] someone who could command the stage and command an audience as he commanded history, and who would bow to no stereotype, and who would in the best sense be a role model not only to blacks and whites, but to all people everywhere."

(Library of Congress)

Marcus Garvey

1 8 8 7 – 1 9 4 0

"Where Is the Black Man's Government?"

ONE

As a child growing up in Jamaica, Marcus Garvey played freely with children of all colors, including whites. He was not an attractive youth—short, squat, almost neckless, with puffy ebony features that led other children to poke fun at him as "Ugly Mug." He only laughed away his hurt until one day when he was fourteen. Then one of his childhood friends, the white daughter of a clergyman, told him she was being sent to Scotland and added coldly that she wanted nothing more to do with him.

"But why?" he asked in bewilderment.

"My parents said I was never to write or get in touch with you any more because you're a nigger."

The cruel word slashed into his heart like a dagger. He never forgot that moment as long as he lived. He burned with rage at the realization that in whites' eyes his black skin made him inferior.

He vowed that he would never again permit himself to be humiliated because of his race. He tried to save other blacks from this indignity, urging his followers to take pride in their African heritage. A quarter of a century after his death, the Black Power movement, his spiritual child, would take up his defiant motto, "Black Is Beautiful!"

MARCUS MOSIAH GARVEY was born August 17, 1887, in Saint Anne's Bay, a little town on the north coast of British Jamaica. His parents, Marcus and Sarah Garvey, were direct descendants of African slaves with no mixed blood. His father, a stonemason, spent much of his earnings on books, educating himself and becoming versed in the law. Marcus's religious mother gave him the middle name of Mosiah, hoping he would grow up to "be like Moses and lead his people."

Browsing in his father's library, Marcus learned about the colonization and partition of Africa by European powers. He became aware of a worldwide pattern of oppression of those with black skin by those with white skin. He saw the same pattern close to home. Because he and his family were pure blacks, they lived on the lowest social and economic level in British Jamaica.

The white man was master by virtue of his color, while those in the highest places under him were light-skinned mulattoes. And the "almost-whites," or mulattoes, exhibited the same disdain for dark black Jamaicans as their white overlords.

Marcus also read with fascination about fiery rebellions by Jamaican slaves before slavery was finally abolished in 1834. He was inspired by stories of the heroic slave leaders who had fought against injustice and won.

Marcus's father died when he was twelve. Because of economic hardships, Marcus was forced to leave school at fourteen and enter an apprenticeship with his godfather, a printer in Kingston.

By the age of twenty Marcus had become a master printer, winning a job as foreman of the island's largest printing firm. He read avidly a weekly paper they printed, *The Jamaica Advocate*, published by a U.S.-educated black priest, Robert Love. Viewing the island's problems through a black prism, Love agitated for black representation on Jamaica's Legislative Council.

Love's ideas strongly influenced Marcus, who grew indignant at the miserable wages and treatment he and other black employees received from the company operating the printshop. Exhorting the workers to rebel, Marcus led them out on strike. The company offered him a raise if he would return and call off the strike. He refused.

The strike failed when the company brought in workers to take the strikers' places. Some of the chastened strikers were taken back, but Marcus was both locked out and blacklisted by all Jamaica's commercial printers.

Marcus had greatly enjoyed the exciting experience of organizing the strike. Perhaps, he mused, he had a unique gift for rallying fellow blacks against exploitation. Toward that end he strove to improve his talents as a speaker. He began organizing local oratorical contests at which he could develop and display his verbal skills.

Encouraged by Robert Love, Marcus decided to appeal to Jamaica's black workers to organize and unite their strength. Throwing caution to the wind, he gave up a new job at a government printshop to start his own political magazine, *Garvey's Watchman*. After it failed, Marcus decided that he needed to get an organization in place first.

He formed the National Club, using membership dues to publish a little fortnightly magazine called *Our Own*. In it Marcus attacked the island's colored caste system. Blacks must not be ashamed of their color, Marcus insisted, but should instead take racial pride in it.

Most black Jamaicans, however, were resigned to the deeply entrenched code that declared "the lighter the better." Despite Marcus's now considerable talents of persuasion, both the National Club and its magazine failed. In disgust, Marcus, now twenty-three, decided to leave for possibly more receptive ears in Costa Rica.

TWO

IN Costa Rica an uncle won Marcus a job as a timekeeper on a banana plantation that hired Jamaican field hands. Marcus was again outraged by flagrant discrimination against black workers, who were paid starvation wages for backbreaking work in sweltering weather and malarial terrain. They were also victims of robbery and murder by local bandits, against whom the government offered no protection.

Bristling at the submissiveness of black field hands to their miserable lot, Marcus tried to organize them with another newspaper, *La Nacionale.* But the Jamaican workers in Costa Rica were terrified of defying their ruthless employer, the United Fruit Company. As the largest employer in Central America, it controlled governments and employed only those peons on its plantations who submitted to miserly wages and miserable conditions. Attempts to strike were crushed with bullets and bludgeons. The company was so powerful that when Guatemalan president Jacobo Arbenz dared confiscate United Fruit Company lands for distribution to the peons, the CIA was ordered to overthrow the Arbenz government and did.

Discouraged when *La Nacionale* also failed, Marcus borrowed money from his uncle and left for Panama. He was still determined to find a way to challenge the prejudice against black skin and to champion the cause of blacks in the Caribbean.

When his fourth paper, *La Prensa,* failed, a disheartened Marcus left Panama. For the next year he traveled and worked in Nicaragua, Honduras, Ecuador, Venezuela, and Colombia. Yet no matter which country he moved to, he saw black workers suffer the same mistreatment and discrimination.

Returning to Jamaica, he made a vigorous protest to the British consul, demanding that the authorities take action to protect Jamaican black workers both at home and abroad. After the consul coolly ignored him, Marcus reached two depressing conclusions: Caribbean whites had no intention of treating blacks humanely, and Caribbean blacks were too downtrodden to rise up in rebellion.

Having failed to make any headway against prejudice in the colonial Caribbean, Marcus now believed he had been too shortsighted in tackling the problem. Color was not just a Caribbean or South American problem. It was a problem wherever blacks labored under a white master race.

He later wrote, "I asked, 'Where is the black man's government? Where is his King and his Kingdom? Where is his President, his country, and his ambassador, his army, his navy, his men of big affairs?' I could not find them; and then I declared, 'I will help to make them.' "

Prejudice was a world blight. Blacks in any one tiny country might be helpless. But if they were united with other blacks all over the world, they could become a powerful force with which the white powers would have to reckon.

Why not, he mused, go to London? At the heart of the British empire he would have a greater opportunity to learn about the condition of millions of blacks in British colonies around the globe. In London he could meet African blacks who could tell him what life was like on their continent and perhaps help him to arouse its great dormant black force.

So in 1912 Marcus emigrated to London. Here he found an editorial job on a monthly magazine called *African Times and Orient Review*. To research his articles and increase his knowledge, he read voraciously in London's libraries. He was deeply impressed by African author Attoh Ahuma, who summoned blacks everywhere: "UP, YOU MIGHTY RACE. YOU CAN ACCOMPLISH WHAT YOU WILL!"

The more Marcus delved into his subject, the more convinced he became that the subjugation and poverty of blacks was the result of powerlessness in a world where might made right. He was intrigued by discovering that time and again, black leaders had sought to inspire an exodus out of countries that oppressed blacks and back to Africa.

The "back to Africa" movement had failed, Marcus reasoned, because the continent was still carved up by colonial powers that kept blacks in subjugation. As long as Africans remained enslaved, what incentive could there be for blacks elsewhere to trade bad for worse? No, he decided, Africa had first to be freed from white colonialism. Only then could it offer a free homeland for all blacks and exert a powerful influence to end racial oppression all over the world.

Two years in London made Marcus passionately anticolonial, antiwhite, and strongly convinced that existing white governments and businesses would not willingly give power to blacks. Now inspired by Booker T. Washington's autobiography, *Up From Slavery*, he returned to Jamaica in 1914 to lead oppressed blacks into their own black enclave where they could find independence and prosperity.

Marcus was not surprised to find little enthusiasm or support for his project from the island's leading mulattoes. "I was a black man and therefore had absolutely no right to lead," he later reported sardonically. "In the opinion of the 'coloured' element, leadership should have been in the hands of a yellow or a very light man. . . . There is more bitterness among us Negroes because of the caste of colour than there is between any other peoples."

Nevertheless, in August 1914, just as World War I broke out, Marcus founded the Universal Negro Improvement Association (UNIA). He urged blacks everywhere to "take Africa, organize it, develop it, arm it, and make it the defender of Negroes the world over." He raised the slogan, "One God! One Aim! One Destiny!"

As he expected, the blacks who joined UNIA were those with the blackest skins. Instilling them with racial pride, he insisted that they not assimilate or associate with whites. Only fully black Negroes who venerated their African heritage, said Marcus, and not the white man's institutions, could be trusted with the struggle for black power.

Marcus became the leader of a black peasantry that previously had no leader because, he charged, "the educated class of my own people . . . are the bitterest enemies of their own race." Although he won a following in Jamaica, the UNIA membership remained small and—owing to long subjugation, malnutrition, and illiteracy—largely apathetic. They considered Marcus's goals hopelessly overoptimistic and unrealistic, with little relevance to their present conditions.

Looking back on this period, he later wrote:

I had to decide whether to please my friends and be one of the "black-whites" of Jamaica, and be reasonably prosperous, or come out openly and defend and help improve and protect the integrity of the black millions and suffer. I decided to do the latter. . . . I was openly hated and persecuted by some of these colored men of the island who did not want to be classified as Negroes, but as white. They hated me worse than poison. They opposed me at every step.

T H R E E

AF T E R two years of struggling to build UNIA, Marcus decided that he needed a larger base of operations to make his
dream flourish. Why not go to the United States?

On March 23, 1916, now almost twenty-nine, he arrived
in New York City accompanied by his secretary, Amy Ashwood. Harlem, one of the great black metropolises of the
world, was in the midst of a population explosion, as thousands of southern blacks moved north for low-paying jobs in
munitions factories. Here Marcus would establish his new
headquarters from which UNIA would rally the "beloved and
scattered millions of the Negro race."

To launch UNIA, Marcus sought the support of Harlem's
black radicals. At first they resented him as a West Indian
intruder. They weren't quite sure what to think about the
pudgy but imposing Jamaican with a wide brow and serious,
penetrating eyes, who identified himself proudly as a "full-
blooded black man."

It was A. Philip Randolph who first gave Marcus a chance
to be heard. A powerful spokesman for black rights, Randolph
had broken with traditional black leaders, openly criticizing
the white government and moderate blacks for not doing
enough to prevent discrimination. His views were considered
so radical, a New York State legislature committee called him
"the most dangerous negro in America."

As Randolph recalled later of Marcus's speaking debut at
his Socialist meeting:

> Someone pulled my coat and said, "There's a young
> man here from Jamaica who wants to be presented to
> this group." I said, "What does he want to talk about?"

He said, "He wants to talk about a movement to develop a back-to-Africa sentiment in America." . . .
Garvey got up on the platform, and you could hear
him from 135th to 125th Street. He had a tremendous
voice.

But Marcus's early street-corner harangues attracted little
attention. Then in June 1917 Hubert H. Harrison, organizer
of a Liberty League of Negro-Americans, became impressed
enough with Marcus to invite him to address a mass meeting
at Harlem's Bethel Church. Marcus recognized the occasion
as his big opportunity and made the most of it.

"This was Harlem's first real sight of Garvey," James Wel-
don Johnson wrote in the *New York Age*, "and his first chance
at Harlem. The man spoke, and his magnetic personality,
torrential eloquence and intuitive knowledge of crowd psy-
chology were all brought into play." Marcus's speech created
a sensation.

Within a month two thousand blacks joined UNIA. The
first members were West Indian immigrants, who strongly
identified with Marcus. Recruiting on Harlem's street corners,
he preached defiantly that "black is beautiful!"

His meetings were soon jammed by enthusiasts who ac-
claimed Marcus's message that blacks of all shades had to
"combine to re-establish the purity of their own race . . .
rather than seeking to lose their identities through miscege-
nation and social intercourse with the white race." He rebuked the mulatto middle class for seeking to "move up and
pass" by marrying whites.

"Any member of this organization who marries a white
woman," Marcus decreed, "is summarily expelled."

Audiences were electrified by his cry, "Africa for the Africans!" He ordered UNIA members to glorify the black past in Africa, where, he promised, someday a great black republic would rise to which blacks all over the world would flock.

But Marcus miscalculated in believing that the racial situation in the United States was the same as in Jamaica. Most American blacks shared a stronger sense of unity, regardless of shade, because of white discrimination against light and dark alike. Many blacks, in fact, approved of light-colored mulattoes passing in white society, convinced they could do more good for the race in the enemy camp.

Understandably, Marcus ran into opposition from many light-skinned leaders of the black community, who saw him as a divisive force. His chief opponent was Dr. W. E. B. Du Bois.

In the NAACP newspaper *Crisis* Du Bois attacked UNIA as a stale revival of old African colonization schemes, all of which had died of "spiritual bankruptcy and futility." While he credited Marcus with sincerity and leadership ability, he considered the "Back to Africa" movement the wrong answer for American blacks.

Nevertheless, increasing thousands of blacks began flocking into UNIA, instilled with the new racial pride Marcus inspired. Proud of his growing success, he had himself elected to head UNIA with the vainglorious title of "President-General."

When America entered World War I in April 1917, the introduction of blacks into the Army and defense plants sparked race riots in East St. Louis and Houston. Those riots, Marcus charged, proved that black Americans could not get fair treatment or justice except by compelling it. "It is advisable," he insisted, "for the Negro to get power of every kind!"

At a mass rally he cried:

Two hundred and fifty years we have been a race of slaves; for fifty years we have been a race of parasites. Now we propose to end all that. No more fear, no more cringing, no more sycophantic begging and pleading; the Negro must strike straight from the shoulder for manhood rights and for full liberty. Destiny leads us to . . . that freedom, that liberty, that will see us men among men, that will make us a great and powerful people.

Marcus helped UNIA grow by editing a weekly, *Negro World*, "the voice of the awakened Negro." It eventually claimed a circulation of one hundred thousand, making it the most widely read black weekly of that day. Following Marcus's policy of glorifying blackness, it refused ads for hair straighteners, skin bleaches, or any product that promised to make the user look whiter. It was the only black publication to reject such ads.

Negro World helped Marcus's influence grow so rapidly that Jamaican poet Claude McKay referred to him as a "Negro Moses" leading his people toward a promised land. While the paper increased Marcus's following, it also provided a forum to challenge his opponents. In it he lashed out at Du Bois as "more of a white man than a Negro," leading mulattoes from an "aristocratic Fifth Avenue office." He derisively lampooned the NAACP as "the National Association for the Advancement of (Certain) Coloured People."

Other black publications joined the duel of words. *The Messenger*, the black Socialist magazine edited by Chandler Owen and A. Philip Randolph, added a personal attack to *Crisis*'s denunciations of UNIA. It described Marcus as "boastful, egotistic, tyrannical, intolerant . . . gifted at self-

White children and parents cheer after the firebombing of a black residence in Chicago, 1919. A wave of race riots, bombings, and lynchings swept the nation after blacks returning from World War I pressed for equality. *(The Bettmann Archive)*

advertisement . . . promising ever, but never fulfilling . . . a lover of pomp, tawdry, finery, and garish display . . . a sheer opportunist and a demagogic charlatan."

Marcus was unruffled by such counterattacks. "Ask me personally the cause of my success," he declared, "and I say opposition; oppose me, and I fight the more!"

FOUR

T H E end of World War I in 1919 brought dramatic changes in race relations in the United States. Black veterans who had served in the "war to make the world safe for democracy" returned home to find that they had won no more of it in their own country. Many blacks, who had first experienced being treated as equals by the English and French, now balked at northern discrimination and southern Jim Crow laws. The result was an increase in racial tensions that swept the country.

The summer of 1919 saw no less than twenty-five major race riots in every part of the country. In one three-day riot, it took three regiments of state militia to halt the violence when blacks tried to integrate a public beach. In Chicago, fifty-eight black families had their homes bombed.

Many popular newspapers and magazines now mirrored hostile white attitudes toward blacks. *Century* magazine featured short stories ridiculing "niggahs" and "darkies." *Harper's* claimed blacks in Charleston were "reverting to the African jungle culture."

With the new black demands for equality spurred by the war, the Ku Klux Klan experienced a huge resurgence, claiming five million members at its peak. The Klan grew so powerful that many eminent southerners felt compelled to join, especially politicians. For a while the Klan dominated the state governments of Texas and Oklahoma, and now chapters began springing up in Midwest and eastern states, including New York. Klan-organized violence toward blacks increased accordingly. In the first year after the war alone, seventy blacks were lynched. In the years that followed, numerous other blacks suffered kidnappings, flogging, mutilation, and murder, yet Klansmen almost never felt the hand of the law.

As black fear of the Klan and disillusionment at outbreaks of naked racism increased, Marcus's message of African redemption reached across the country. He dared exhort southern blacks in a speaking tour through the South, but only after a machine gun had been mounted on the roof of his car. UNIA's membership soared above the two million mark as blacks flooded into its ranks to regain lost dignity and self-respect.

Following his separatist policy, Marcus created a corps of Black Cross nurses and a Black Eagle Flying Corps. Black children were told to play only with black dolls. And why, Marcus demanded, wasn't there also a Black House in Washington? He asked his followers to think only of a black God and a black Jesus when they worshiped. Wasn't man made in the image of God? Why, then, worship a white deity when you were a black person?

Stressing UNIA's links to Africa, Marcus organized an African Orthodox Church as well as an African Legion. With racial purity as his banner, he promised to lead his followers back to Africa to establish a great nation of their own.

Planning to transport them there, Marcus considered it unthinkable to use white steamship lines, with their policy of discrimination. He decided to launch a spectacular enterprise, the Black Star Steamship Line, "to own, charter, operate, and navigate ships of various types in any part of the world and to carry passengers, freight and mails."

Through the mail he offered blacks the opportunity to become shareholders in this new big business enterprise. Stock was offered for as little as $5 a share, giving poor blacks a chance to be partners, and limiting the number of shares any one person could own to two hundred.

Sociologist Gunnar Myrdal reported that UNIA was the first organized black protest movement that really gripped the imagination and enthusiasm of the black American masses. As one woman UNIA member said fervently, "Garvey is giving my people backbones where they had wishbones."

Meanwhile, Marcus's growing success as an antiwhite agitator worried the FBI. In 1919 J. Edgar Hoover was then a young FBI zealot who suspected every radical, liberal, and trade union leader of being actual or unwitting Russian agents conspiring to overthrow the United States.

Hoover wrote in a memo:

Garvey is a West Indian Negro who [has] been particularly active among the radical elements in New York City agitating the Negro movement. Unfortunately, however, he has not as yet violated any federal law whereby he could be proceeded against on the grounds of being an undesirable alien, from the view of deportation. It occurs to me, however . . . that there might be some proceeding against him for fraud in connection with his Black Star Line propaganda.

A subsequent mistake with Black Star Line stock offerings gave the racist Hoover the opportunity he wanted to ruin Garvey.

———————

F I V E

M A R C U S promoted sales of Black Star stock by declaring, "Ask Rockefeller where he came from, ask Carnegie where he came from . . . and they will tell you that they came from the lowly places of life; they started out with the dollar, and then made the ten dollars and, after, the millions. Man, do not beg and remain idle, but borrow a dollar or beg a dollar and start your career today."

The money poured in. Most blacks who invested were convinced of the bright future Marcus painted of a booming, free African homeland, which would become to blacks what the opening of the West had been to poor eastern whites.

In the fall of 1919 Marcus went to Chicago, following its devastating race riot. He had just bought the first ship of the Black Star Line, a rusting thirty-two-year-old freighter that Garvey renamed the S.S. *Frederick Douglass.* Proudly announcing its purchase, he urged Chicago blacks to buy Black Star Line stock and plan for an African future with UNIA.

"There is no manhood future in the United States for the Negro . . ." he told them. "The whites will not grant social equality to the Negroid race. . . . I believe that two or three million of us should return to the land of our ancestors, and establish our own nation, civilization, laws, customs, style of manufacture."

However, Marcus began to run into trouble when Robert S. Abbott, black publisher and editor of the *Chicago Defender,* labeled UNIA and the Black Star Line fraudulent schemes promoted by Marcus for his own benefit. Marcus sued him for libel and won, only to be countersued by Abbott after Marcus called him a "traitor to his race."

More trouble arose when Marcus sold stock certificates

in the Black Star Line, in violation of certain Illinois laws on stock sales, to a black detective posing as an investor. Arrested and freed on bail, Marcus left Chicago and did not return to stand trial. He blamed Abbott for engineering his arrest out of rivalry and jealousy.

Marcus considered the Chicago difficulties behind him when he returned to New York. In October 1919, while he was in his Harlem office, a black named George Tyler rushed in shouting, "I come to get you!" He fired a pistol three times. Though Marcus's secretary, Amy Ashwood, whom he soon married, rushed the gunman and spoiled his aim, one shot hit Marcus in the leg and another creased his scalp. Office assistants seized Tyler, holding him until the police arrived.

Tyler never went to trial because police reported that while in custody he had "fallen or leaped" to his death. His motive for the attempted assassination remained unclear, although Marcus hinted darkly about "certain enemies."

The resulting press coverage, featuring pictures of Marcus on crutches with his head bandaged, attracted thousands more blacks into UNIA. Using the publicity to advantage, Marcus founded UNIA's Negro Factories Corporation to "build and operate factories in the big industrial centers of the United States, Central America, the West Indies and Africa to manufacture every marketable commodity." Marcus now dreamed of building an entire self-sufficient black world economy, free of dependence on white companies.

Working hard at building UNIA, Marcus made the grandiose claim at the height of its growth that it numbered eleven million members. Later investigation indicated that it had never enlisted more than a hundred thousand actual members, mostly in the large northern cities, although an estimated six million blacks at one time did support Marcus.

In the spring of 1920 Marcus bought two more vessels for the Black Star Line. One was used to give New York UNIA members recreational excursions up the Hudson River. Unfortunately for Marcus, all three UNIA vessels proved to be unseaworthy, needing expensive repairs. Worse, the financial arrangements paying for them were found inadequate. It became apparent that Marcus's knowledge of business and finance left a great deal to be desired, a problem compounded by his stubborn, egoistic refusal to listen to or take expert advice.

While the ships purchased for Marcus's Back to Africa movement were unsound, he did have a more realistic plan for the black emigration. Knowing the impossibility of a wholesale migration to all of the continent, he focused on developing Liberia, which was already a free state, and settling his followers there. He wrote a letter to Liberia's president, Charles D. B. King, in May 1920, outlining his plan.

The letter was carried to Liberia by Black Star Line secretary Elie Garcia. Garcia received the assurances Marcus wanted from Liberia's president. But then Garcia mailed a confidential report to Marcus that bluntly described Liberia as a poor country with a lazy work force, a caste system, and corrupt bureaucrats.

"They are absolutely hostile to immigration by American or West Indian Negroes," Garcia wrote, "that is, if said Negroes show any tendency to take part in the political life of the Republic. This fact is of great importance. . . . [We need] to deny firmly any intention on our part to enter into politics in Liberia. This attitude . . . will not prevent us after having a strong foothold in the country to act as we see best for their own betterment and that of the Race at large."

Unfortunately for Marcus, this volatile memo was intercepted by Liberian officials, with disastrous results.

SIX

MEANWHILE, in August 1920 Marcus prepared to stage a first International Convention of the Negro People of the World in New York City. It took place in a grand manner, impressing New Yorkers with the power of a huge black organization that only four years earlier had consisted of just one black Jamaican with grandiose aspirations. Black delegations attended from all over the world, a testament to how far Marcus's fame now reached.

A UNIA parade began in Harlem, led by thousands of its "African Legion" in blue uniforms with red trouser stripes, followed by a corps of one hundred Black Cross nurses dressed in white. Fifty thousand black marchers proudly carried UNIA banners, with slogans such as ONE GOD! ONE AIM! ONE DESTINY! and FREE AFRICA!

The grand marshal of the parade was a dignified fat black man in a splendid braided uniform and magnificent purple and gold feathered helmet—thirty-three-year-old UNIA President-General Marcus Garvey himself. It was the proudest moment of his life. He drank in the heady acclaim of thousands of admiring blacks who cheered the leader once sneered at as "Ugly Mug" and "nigger."

A young black boy, James H. Robinson, who watched the parade later grew up to found Operation Crossroads Africa. "Marcus Garvey," he recalled, "captured the imagination of thousands, because he personified the possibility of a dream latent in the heart of every Negro. . . . When Garvey swept by in his plumed hat, I got an emotional lift, which swept me up above the poverty and the prejudice by which my life was limited."

Marcus's enthusiastic followers marched all the way

from Harlem to Madison Square Garden, which filled to overflowing to hear him. His international convention was also attended by an African prince and some tribal chiefs, who joined in singing the UNIA anthem, "Ethiopia, Thou Land of Our Fathers."

There were deafening cheers when Marcus unfurled a new UNIA flag—red ("for Negro blood"), black ("for Negro skin"), and green ("for Negro hopes"). One day, he thundered, this tricolor would fly over a free and united Africa.

By acclamation he was proclaimed "provisional president of Africa"—a black Moses who promised to lead his oppressed race out of bondage all over the world to a new black Holy Land that would be theirs alone. The huge crowd roared in pride at Marcus's announcement that their Back to Africa movement already numbered four million followers.

The press took note of Marcus's spectacular parade and convention. Some papers mocked his plans as grandiose and unrealistic. W. E. B. Du Bois continued his attacks, calling Marcus "either a lunatic or a traitor." Stung, Marcus accused Du Bois, who had some French forebears, of being a racist who considered himself superior to Marcus because Marcus had only pure African ancestry.

Other papers gave a more positive report. Black Brooklyn minister G. Miller was quoted in the *Brooklyn Eagle* as saying, "Garvey is the most remarkable man of our times. He may be laughed at and ridiculed, but he has done more to emphasize the restlessness of the black people than any other man."

To sell more Black Star Line stock, Marcus toured the West Indies and Central America in February 1921. Secretary of State Charles Evans Hughes worried about Marcus's ability to stir up black workers on American-owned plantations. Marcus's paper *Negro World* had already been banned in the

Marcus Garvey presides at a Universal Negro Improvement Association (UNIA) parade. With his flamboyant uniform and magnificently plumed hat, Garvey personified his defiant cry, "Black is beautiful!" *(UPI/Bettmann)*

West Indies. Now Hughes cabled U.S. consuls in those countries to deny Marcus himself entry. Marcus nevertheless managed to get into the banana republics and was welcomed by
huge turnouts of blacks who now listened to him eagerly,
cheered his speeches, and bought shares. His reception as the
dynamic head of UNIA was a far cry from the indifference he
had met during his visits seven years earlier.

In August, Marcus organized a parade for the second International Convention of the Negro People of the World in
New York City, which again stirred great enthusiasm in the
black community. But now some clouds were beginning to
gather on the horizon.

Marcus was running into trouble with his operation of
the Black Star Line, in which forty thousand blacks had
bought shares. None of the three old ships he had acquired
ever made a trip to Africa, and all three were seized or sold
to satisfy debts of $750,000. The Negro Factories Corporation
never developed more than a few groceries, laundries, and a
print shop, all of which also failed. Business management,
clearly, was not one of Marcus's unique talents. And worse
was to follow.

In 1922, at the age of thirty-five, he was indicted for mail
fraud for selling stock in the bankrupt Black Star Line. Behind
the indictment was undoubtedly J. Edgar Hoover's determination three years earlier to get something on Marcus and
deport him as an "undesirable alien." Released on bail, Marcus determined to refuse legal counsel at his trial, representing
himself in the belief that the simple truth would vindicate him.

Meanwhile, further trouble beset him when his marriage
to Amy Ashwood broke up in 1922 over an affair with his
assistant, Amy's young friend Amy Jacques. The court fight
with his wife created a scandal, and the anti-Garvey press lost

no time in lashing him for immoral behavior. But the "immoral" Marcus married Amy Jacques and remained with her for twenty-seven more years, the rest of his life.

His ex-wife later said of Marcus, "Like the rest of us, he was made of mortal clay and he carried his full burden of human weakness and limitation. His chief failing was his inability to share responsibility. He was autocratic, vain, and he loved to hog the spotlight. He erred in trying to shine too brightly."

Believing that his black opponents—the black middle class and the NAACP—had engineered his indictment, Marcus decided to outwit them. Since they refused to support him, he mused, why not get some powerful white support behind him instead? The idea was not as preposterous as it seemed at first glance. After all, what his enemies sought was integration, the very goal the white power structure fought bitterly. And wasn't what *he* wanted—racial purity and black emigration to Africa—the very same things the white power structure ardently desired?

So Marcus made one of the biggest mistakes of his life.

S E V E N

MARCUS went to New Orleans and met with Edward Young Clarke, imperial wizard of the Ku Klux Klan. After listening to him, Clarke invited him to address a Klan conclave.

"This is a white man's country," Marcus told them. "He found it, he conquered it, and we can't blame him if he wants to keep it. I am not vexed with the white man of the south for Jim Crowing me because I am black. I never built any street cars or railroads. The white man built them for his convenience. And if I don't want to ride where he's willing to let me ride, then I'd better walk."

Apologists for Marcus explained hastily that he had simply meant to challenge blacks to build their own infrastructure. But his opponents immediately charged him with aligning himself with the worst persecutors of the black race, hoping to get the Ku Klux Klan to finance his Black Star Line.

The uproar caused a split in the ranks of UNIA. West Indians stubbornly defended Marcus, while Afro-Americans were outraged by what they considered his racial betrayal. Marcus stunned both factions by suddenly resigning as president-general of UNIA.

"I refuse to associate any longer," he declared in August 1922, "with a body of men on the executive council who are not honest enough to do business aboveboard. I am tired of this plotting and intrigue." Loyal officers of UNIA resigned with him.

James W. H. Eason, a former Philadelphia clergyman, was elected UNIA's new leader. Marcus angrily accused him of trying to ruin both Marcus and UNIA. Eason charged that Marcus had only resigned as a ruse, expecting the membership to reelect him. The two men almost came to blows.

Eason offered to testify as a witness for the prosecution at Marcus's trial for mail fraud. But before the trial took place, Eason was shot to death in a New Orleans alley. Marcus, reelected in his place, hotly denied that either he or any supporter in UNIA had a hand in the murder.

The trial of Marcus and three codefendants for fraud opened in New York's federal court on May 18, 1923. The arrogant and incompetent manner in which Marcus conducted his own defense antagonized the court. But one of the witnesses against him told Marcus on the witness stand, "You impress me even now. I have read many evil things about you, but to be candid, I don't believe half of them, even now."

The prosecutor, however, asked the all-white jury, "Shall we let the tiger free?" The jury dismissed the codefendants but found "the tiger" guilty. Marcus was sentenced to five years in a federal prison and fined $1,000. But for three years he managed to stay out on bail by a series of appeals.

Meanwhile, questions arose as to how fair a trial he had received. UCLA history professor Robert Hill revealed years later that the FBI had evidence clearly exonerating Marcus, but had deliberately suppressed it. Marcus's constitutional rights had also been violated when his records, books, and documents, seized illegally by the prosecution, were admitted as evidence over his protests. A brief filed by lawyers after the trial cited ninety-four trial errors that should have resulted in a mistrial.

At his first speech to UNIA after his release on bail, Marcus insisted that he had not really been tried and convicted for fraud, but for having the audacity to seek to free blacks from the oppression of white America.

"I was convicted," he charged, "because an atmosphere of hostility was created around me. I was convicted because wicked enemies, malicious and jealous members of my own race, misrepresented me to those in authority for the purpose of discrediting and destroying me. . . . Negroes who, for the sake of position and privilege, will sell their own mothers."

The Richmond, Virginia, *Planet* deplored Marcus's harsh sentence and accused the federal government of persecuting him with repressive measures because of prejudice against black radicals. Even Marcus's adversary Du Bois admitted, "He has been charged with dishonesty and graft, but he seems to me essentially an honest and sincere man with a tremendous vision, great dynamic force, stubborn determination and unselfish desire to serve."

Marcus, meanwhile, renewed his efforts to go forward with his UNIA plan to settle its membership in Liberia. To thwart him, the NAACP persuaded President Calvin Coolidge to appoint Du Bois "ambassador extraordinary" to Liberia, to attend the second inaugural of President King. Coolidge was advised that this move would help assure NAACP support for the Republicans, while Du Bois' opposition to UNIA would cut the ground out from under Marcus.

Despite his acknowledgment of Marcus's integrity, Du Bois wrote in the *Crisis*, "Marcus Garvey is, without doubt, the most dangerous enemy of the Negro race in America and the world."

Marcus was also viewed as the most dangerous enemy of powerful American and European interests that controlled Liberian rubber, iron ore, and diamonds, as well as of the colonial powers that milked other colonies on the African continent.

U.S. Assistant Secretary of State William Castle advised Liberia that UNIA was considered by the United States to be a Communist organization, despite the fact that Marcus had vehemently fought communism, calling its black proponents "Red Uncle Toms." Britain and France also protested Marcus's plans for Liberia and banned *Negro World* in many of their territories in Africa and the Americas. The Western powers' opposition added fuel to the anger already aroused among Liberian officials by their earlier interception of the derogatory report sent to Marcus by his envoy Elie Garcia.

Liberia slammed the door shut on recognition for Marcus. Washington was informed that Liberia was "irrevocably opposed both in principle and in fact to the incendiary policy

William E. B. Du Bois, a co-founder of the National Association for the Advancement of Colored People (NAACP), was one of Garvey's most vocal critics, attacking Garvey as "either a lunatic or a traitor." *(Courtesy NAACP)*

of the Universal Negro Improvement Association headed by Marcus Garvey."

Marcus, however, was not informed of this development. Early in 1924 he sent seven experts to Liberia to build temporary housing for UNIA colonists who would follow. They were promptly arrested upon arrival and deported. Some $50,000 worth of building materials they had brought with them were confiscated.

Marcus's last real chance to establish an African homeland had vanished.

EIGHT

MARCUS was embittered by what he considered an attempt by white society to victimize him for rejecting an inferior role for blacks through his Back to Africa movement. Seeking to spread his message of black rebellion, he wrote a book called *The Philosophy and Opinions of Marcus Garvey*.

"We are organized not to hate other men," he wrote, "but to lift ourselves, and to demand respect of all humanity. . . . Men of the Negro race, let me say to you that a greater future is in store for us; we have no cause to lose hope, to become faint-hearted. . . . We are determined that we shall have a free country . . . a flag . . . a government, second to none."

Demanding that whites stop beating, brutalizing, killing, burning, imprisoning, and scorning blacks, he warned, "It may come back to you one of these fine days."

He reminded his racial brothers that when Europe had been inhabited by savages, Africa had had sophisticated cultures: "Black men, you were once great; you shall be great again. . . . Get organized, and you will compel the world to respect you." Unless the white world did, he predicted grimly,

"Four hundred millions of you shall, through organization, shake the pillars of the universe and bring down creation, even as Samson brought down the temple upon his head and the heads of the Philistines."

Shaking off his rebuff from Liberia, Marcus organized a parade for the fourth International UNIA Convention of the Negro People of the World. He stunned and delighted on-lookers by featuring in the parade a large portrait of a black Madonna and child.

On February 2, 1925, the last appeal of his sentence was rejected. Marcus was seized by U.S. marshals in a Harlem station as his train arrived, and was rushed off in handcuffs. Sent to the federal penitentiary in Atlanta, he felt apprehensive that he would not emerge alive. He sent a message to his followers that appeared in *Negro World:*

"Look for me in the whirlwind or the song of the storm, look for me all around you, for with God's grace I shall come and bring with me the countless millions of black slaves who have died in America and the West Indies and the millions in Africa to aid you in the fight for liberty."

Marcus's life in prison was hard and the duties he was given were always the dirtiest—the result of his enemies' influence with the deputy warden.

"But I philosophically accepted the duties," he wrote later, "and executed them to the best of my ability." In a little while the warden learned of his deputy's treatment of Marcus and transferred Marcus to easier and better tasks.

Marcus asked a steady stream of visitors and newsmen to pressure politicians for a pardon. He accused a conspiracy of black politicians and organizations, government officials, the United Fruit Company, and his former wife, Amy Ashwood, of seeking to destroy him and UNIA. But a pardon was denied him on grounds that Marcus was "a dangerous race agitator."

Even though he himself was behind bars, his dream of a new free Africa and a new free black race persisted.

"It was a grandiose and bombastic scheme, utterly impracticable as a whole, but it was sincere and had some practical features," admitted his foe W. E. B. Du Bois. "And Garvey proved not only an astonishing popular leader, but a master of propaganda. Within a few years, news of his movement, of his promise and plans, reached Europe and Asia, and penetrated every corner of Africa."

When the fifth UNIA Convention of the Negro People of the World met in August 1926 with Marcus still in prison, its secretary declared, "We still respect Garvey as the man who gave the idea for the African program, but we admit at the same time as a business man he is a failure. We feel that the association needs most at this time an economic program which we are not willing to submit to Marcus Garvey."

Those UNIA members and other blacks who considered Marcus a race martyr, vengefully and excessively punished for his opposition to the white world, campaigned persistently for his release. Finally, on November 28, 1927, after serving two years and nine months in prison, pressure by black leaders and white liberals led to Marcus's sentence being commuted by President Coolidge. He was not allowed to visit UNIA headquarters in New York, but was immediately deported from New Orleans to Kingston, Jamaica, as an "undesirable alien."

N I N E

M A R C U S received a hero's welcome back in his homeland. Undaunted by his fall, he began reviving UNIA chapters in the Caribbean and Central America. Then he and his second wife, Amy Jacques, left for Europe to open a London head-quarters.

But there the fervor of his message was lost on the British, who were not partial to black activism. A mass meeting he called to launch a campaign for justice to blacks in British colonies got only a disappointing turnout. Nevertheless, he exerted considerable influence on the growth of African nationalism through his contacts with Africans studying in London as well as through his writings.

Returning to Kingston, in March 1929 he founded another weekly, *The Black Man*. In it Marcus announced the sixth International Convention of the Negro People of the World, to take place in Kingston. The convention began with the usual flamboyant parade. In his speech Marcus accused leaders of New York's UNIA of ruining the movement while he had been in prison.

Since UNIA had been founded by Marcus, his followers agreed that its headquarters should be wherever he was. A split occurred, the New Yorkers continuing with their organization, while Marcus's followers stayed with him.

Now he decided that the time was ripe to make his move in Jamaican politics. Organizing a People's Political Party, he called for reform of the island's legislative council. He demanded greater participation by, and protection for, Jamaica's poor blacks. The council ordered Marcus seized, sentenced to three months in jail, and fined a hundred pounds. While he was imprisoned, his followers elected him to a seat on the council.

Marcus's attempt to force reforms in Jamaica was quickly nullified when the Depression spread from the United States to the Caribbean. The American UNIA also suffered and, without Marcus's electrifying presence, gradually expired.

Marcus's own following dwindled, and he gradually found himself becoming a pathetic figure—a forgotten and neglected leader. Young children ran behind him in Kingston's streets, taunting him with their parents' insults. It was said that he was becoming an embarrassment to his associates and that they had bought him passage to London to be rid of him.

In any event, in 1935 Marcus took his family to London, where he continued publishing *The Black Man*. Without a UNIA organization to herd audiences for him, he was reduced to speaking at Hyde Park's open-air meetings, where he became a regular Sunday soapbox attraction. When Italian dictator Mussolini's forces invaded African Ethiopia, Marcus's fiery denunciations helped arouse Londoners' indignation.

In the late thirties Marcus organized new regional UNIA conferences in Toronto, Canada, where he set up a UNIA leadership school for blacks called the School of African Philosophy.

In 1937 he made a final tour of the West Indies, except for Jamaica, speaking to large and enthusiastic crowds everywhere. Despite his misfortunes, the name of Garvey was still magic among blacks. He was even now feared by British foreign office officials, who at first barred him from Trinidad, which was experiencing labor unrest, but relented on condition he neither hold any outdoor meetings nor make any political speeches.

Returning to London, he was trapped there by the outbreak of World War II, which prevented him from visiting his family, who were now settled in Jamaica.

Ailing at age fifty-three, thousands of miles from his homeland and family, Marcus suffered a stroke in January 1940. He died on June 10, worn out from a lifetime of struggle in pursuit of his elusive dream.

TEN

HARLEM called a mass meeting to mourn Marcus's passing.

Five years later a three-day International Convention of the Negro People of the World was held in Harlem on Marcus's birthday, at which speakers from Liberia, Nigeria, the West Indies, and the United States hailed his memory.

Although Marcus Garvey had attracted the allegiance of the masses of black people more than any other black leader up to that time, the weakness of his movement was that his followers could do little more than join UNIA and invest in its enterprises. His program failed to stir blacks to direct action, as later black militant movements succeeded in doing.

"The practical prospect of Garvey's actually physically transporting blacks back to Africa turned most black people off," Black Panther leader Eldridge Cleaver observed later, "because of a world situation and balance of power that made such a solution impossible."

But if Marcus made mistakes, he also contributed tremendously to the growth of black pride, black unity, and black power. His rebellion was principally a psychological crusade to arouse the slumbering race consciousness of blacks everywhere, bringing the desperately needed message that blackness was a badge of honor, not shame. He had demanded complete separation from whites, which he felt could only be achieved by returning to the black motherland—Africa. And he had built the largest mass movement of blacks ever won by a black leader.

His teachings greatly influenced Ghana's president, Kwame Nkrumah, who declared, "Of all the literature I stud-

Marcus Garvey, center, leaves court handcuffed to a U.S. marshal in 1925. Garvey was sentenced to five years in federal prison for mail fraud; after serving two years and nine months, he was released and deported to Jamaica. *(UPI/Bettmann)*

ied, the book that did more than any other to fire my enthusiasm was *The Philosophy and Opinions of Marcus Garvey.*" Nkrumah named Ghana's own steamship company the Black Star Line and praised Marcus as the spiritual father of Ghana, the first black republic in the new Africa emerging from colonialism.

When his native Jamaica became independent of England in 1962, at independence ceremonies Marcus was proclaimed one of the island's national heroes. His remains were transferred from London to a black star-shaped tomb in Jamaica that was ordained a national shrine.

The Daily Gleaner, which upon Marcus's arrival back in Jamaica in 1924 had called him "a Jamaican for whom the island as a whole or the more intelligent sector of it has no use," now called the return of the body "welcome news for all Jamaicans." It added, "It is difficult not to ponder on the changes in the outlook of the Jamaican people since Marcus Garvey stumped the streets of Harlem."

Marcus's stirring of racial identity was followed in the United States by what became known as the Harlem Renaissance—an emergence of black writers who fostered black culture, like Langston Hughes, Claude McKay, and Richard Wright. Hughes declared, "We younger Negro artists who create now intend to express our individual dark-skinned selves without fear or shame."

Representative Adam Clayton Powell, the most influential black man ever to sit in Congress, also credited Marcus Garvey with having shaped much of his thinking.

Even in death Marcus remained controversial. His enemies continued to deride his memory, calling him a charlatan and a buffoon. But Professor Albert Bushnell Hart of Harvard pointed out, "Had Garvey succeeded in his undertakings he would have been uncontestably the greatest figure of the twentieth century. Having failed, he is considered a fool."

The Black Muslim, Black Power, and Black Panther movements of the sixties and seventies, however, elevated Marcus's place in black history. Celebrations of Marcus Garvey Day have been held in Harlem and Jamaica to commemorate the rebel who more than any other black man gave the mass of blacks everywhere a sense of racial pride. It was Marcus's challenge that inspired future generations of black leaders to demand total equality of civil rights with white Americans.

For many blacks the spirit of Marcus Garvey lives on. In 1987, marking the one-hundredth anniversary of his birth, Harlem's Center for Research in Black Culture staged an exhibit: "Marcus Garvey: the Centennial Exhibition." A *New Yorker* reporter wrote, "Today, there are a lot of people who think Garvey's still alive. . . . I was conducting radio interviews with some young Rastafarians, who look to Garvey as their prophet . . . and realized they were quietly laughing behind me. One of them said, 'That man think Marcus Garvey dead.' They felt pity for me. I was uninformed. In black folk culture, there is no death for the righteous."

Today American blacks who wear African-style clothing and Afro hairstyles are, in effect, also paying tribute to Marcus Garvey, who ironically never once laid eyes upon, nor set foot on, the Africa of his dreams.

(Library of Congress)

Martin Luther King, Jr.

1929 – 1968

"I Have a Dream"

ONE

In October 1960 some seventy-five black college students, members of the Student Nonviolent Coordinating Committee (SNCC), decided to risk demanding service at a segregated restaurant in Atlanta's biggest department store. They would refuse to leave until they were served. A picket line outside the store was planned to protest its Jim Crow policy.

The students knew they would need a famous name with them if they hoped to win national publicity for their dangerous defiance of southern segregation. They appealed to the Reverend Martin Luther King, Jr., to join their challenge.

Martin did not hesitate. He carried a sign on the picket line, then went inside and sat down with the students. When they refused to leave without service, police were called. They were all arrested and trundled off to jail.

After a week in jail Martin was released. But just as soon as he emerged, he was rearrested by the sheriff of De Kalb County, a Ku Klux Klan stronghold, on a trumped-up charge. Sentenced to six months of hard labor in the state penitentiary at Reidsville, Georgia, he was taken there in handcuffs and leg chains.

When wire services reported the arrest of the famous black civil rights leader, a little white girl sneered to Martin's five-year-old daughter Yoki, "Oh, your daddy is *always* going to jail!"

"Yes," Yoki replied proudly, "he goes to jail to help people."

Born on January 29, 1929, Martin grew up the son of one of the most influential black Baptist preachers in America. Although he initially rebelled at following in his father's footsteps, he seemed destined for the ministry like his grandfather and father before him. Under slavery the ministry had been the only white-collar trade open to blacks. For the following century it still remained the most desirable black path to security and prestige.

Growing up in Atlanta surrounded by WHITES ONLY signs, Martin became aware of his father's determined resistance to racism. Once while riding in his father's car, he listened as a traffic policeman stopped Martin, Sr., for a minor traffic violation.

"Look here, boy—" the cop drawled.

The minister stopped him short, pointing to Martin, Jr.

"*That* is a boy," he snapped. "*I* am a man."

On another occasion, when Martin's father was buying him shoes, the store clerk ordered them to move to the rear of the store or he would not serve them. Martin, Sr., informed the clerk bluntly that they would either buy shoes just where they sat, or not at all.

Martin's mother, Alberta, often worried that her husband's resistance to Jim Crow laws would land him or the family in serious trouble. At the same time she impressed upon Martin, Jr., that "one man can make a difference" and encouraged him to make the most of his talents.

At six Martin suffered the same kind of rejection Marcus Garvey had experienced. He had a white playmate he considered a close friend until the day his friend's mother came to the door and told him he could not come around anymore. Shocked by being considered inferior simply because his skin was black, Martin wept about it to his mother.

"Don't let this thing impress you," she told him. "Don't let it make you feel you're not as good as white people. You're as good as anyone else, and don't you forget it!"

But when he was eleven, Martin had a second traumatic experience in a department store. A white woman suddenly slapped his face, shouting, "You're the little nigger who stepped on my foot!"

Martin's belief in the value of being articulate showed itself at an early age. Aroused by the eloquence of a visiting preacher, Martin told his mother, "Someday I'm going to have me some big words like that!" He set to work developing his vocabulary.

Martin's verbal ability came in handy in the schoolyard and on the streets of Atlanta. At first when bullied by bigger children, he fought back furiously and gave a good account of himself. But after a while he grew tired of getting bruised and battered for no good reason and learned to talk his way out of confrontations, an ability that would serve him well in the future.

His father gave Martin and his siblings no allowance, telling them to work for whatever they wanted. Martin took a job as a newsboy, earning the money he used to buy dressy clothes and books about black history. He was eager to learn more about his racial ancestry and just why white people insisted upon discriminating against blacks. Reading about famous figures like Nat Turner, Denmark Vesey, George Washington Carver, and Frederick Douglass, he was fascinated by their struggles against oppression.

At eleven Martin attended an experimental school run by Atlanta University. There he developed his vocabulary extensively, becoming an effective speaker. He began to compete in oratorical contests, winning first prize after his transfer to Washington High School for his speech entitled "The Negro and the Constitution."

One of these contests took Martin and some black class-

Jackie Robinson became the first black baseball player in the
major leagues when the Brooklyn Dodgers hired him in 1947.
Although segregation and discrimination were still the norm,
Robinson inspired other blacks to join him in the world of
professional sports. *(UPI/Bettmann Newsphotos)*

mates to Valdosta. On the bus ride home, the driver forced them to give up their seats to white passengers boarding the bus. They had to stand for the whole ninety minutes back to Atlanta.

"It was a night I'll never forget," Martin later recalled. "I don't think I have ever been so deeply angry in my life."

T W O

A s a high school junior, Martin went north with a few classmates for summer work as laborers on a Connecticut tobacco farm, earning money for college tuition. The experience of his first travel out of the South opened Martin's eyes. He found it incredibly liberating to be free of all the whites-only restrictions of Georgia.

Why, he wondered, shouldn't blacks in the South also be able to go to any theaters or restaurants of their choice? He daydreamed that one day his oratory might compel the removal of legal restrictions against blacks in his home state.

Educationally advanced for his age, at fifteen he was allowed to enter Morehouse College while continuing to live at home. Thoreau's essay *On Civil Disobedience* made a tremendous impression on him. He felt inspired to use this technique to defy the prejudicial laws of the South. Despite his inclination to resist the pressures of his father, Martin decided that the best way to accomplish his newly found purpose was by spreading his message from the pulpit.

When Martin was only seventeen, his father gave him an opportunity to deliver his first sermon. After hearing Martin speak, his impressed father kneeled to thank God for giving him such an eloquent son. Only one year later Martin was ordained a full minister and was made an assistant pastor in his father's church.

Upon graduating from Morehouse, he was given a scholarship to the Crozer Theological Seminary at Chester, Pennsylvania, to earn a master's degree in philosophy. Although only one of six blacks among one hundred students, Martin was determined not to allow himself to be stigmatized. He wrote later:

I was well aware of the typical white stereotype of the Negro, that he is always late, that he's loud and always laughing, that he's dirty and messy, and for a while I was terribly conscious of trying to avoid identification with it. If I were a minute late to class, I was almost morbidly conscious of it and sure that everyone else noticed it. Rather than be thought of as always laughing, I'm afraid I was grimly serious at the time.

At Crozer Martin became first in his class and president of the student body. Possible envy and racism drove one southern white student to point a gun at Martin and falsely accuse him of trashing his room. When the irate student was disarmed, Martin refused to press charges.

Martin was excited by a lecture on the great Indian leader Mahatma Gandhi and his nonviolent resistance against political injustice. Buying books on Gandhi, Martin devoured them eagerly. An inspiration seized him. Why not combine the teachings of Gandhi, Thoreau, and Jesus Christ to combat unjust laws against blacks? Martin felt confident he could persuade blacks to break prejudicial laws, then allow themselves to be arrested and jailed as martyrs.

The secret weapon of blacks, he would preach, should be love instead of hate, transforming white hearts.

Graduating from Crozer in 1951, Martin entered Boston University to earn his doctorate. Here he met a young black woman, Coretta Scott, an Alabama storekeeper's daughter studying to be a concert singer. Her first impression of Martin was unfavorable—"How short he seems. How unimpressive he looks." But before their first date was over, Coretta recalled thinking, "He radiated charm. When he talked, he grew in stature."

Even at Martin's young age, Coretta observed, "He drew people to him from the very first moment by his eloquence, his sincerity, and his *moral* stature. I knew immediately that he was very special." As for Martin, on that first date he told her, "You have everything I want in a wife . . . character, intelligence, personality, and beauty."

When he brought Coretta to Atlanta to meet his father, the older King was cool to Martin's choice. He had another local girl in mind for Martin. Coretta, in turned, disliked Martin, Sr., recognizing him as a strong man who sought to dominate his son. She knew that if she married Martin, she would have to fight his father to keep his hands off their marriage and Martin's future.

Despite misgivings by both Coretta and Martin, Sr., the marriage took place on June 18, 1953. Years later Martin, Sr., admitted, "I don't believe there was any girl who could have fitted into Martin's life as Coretta did. No other could have gone through what she did with him and afterward."

As the newlyweds finished their studies in Boston in 1954, the *Brown v. Board of Education* verdict of the Supreme Court required the South to integrate its schools. White Citizens Councils immediately sprang up to stop this from happening, resulting in outbreaks of white violence against southern blacks.

Watching this racial whirlwind in dismay, Martin and Coretta were tempted to stay north, especially when Martin was offered a parish there. But he felt strongly called to return south at once because, he told Coretta, "that is where I am needed."

THREE

MARTIN accepted an offer by the Dexter Avenue Baptist Church parish in Montgomery, Alabama. Here he became friends with young Ralph Abernathy, pastor of the First Baptist Church, who was to become his lifelong colleague in the civil rights movement.

One of the facts of life in Montgomery that both ministers found disturbing was the way in which the Montgomery city bus lines operated. Although 70 percent of its passengers were black, they were treated contemptuously. The front seats were reserved for whites, even when empty, and the backseats were left for blacks. If whites boarded and their section was filled, blacks in the rear were forced to yield their seats. Blacks had to pay fares at the front of the bus, then dismount and walk to the rear door to board again. Sometimes the bus driver enjoyed a "practical joke" by driving off before they could reboard. The white drivers called black passengers "niggers," "black cows," "black apes," and, no matter what a man's age was, "boy."

In March 1955 a fifteen-year-old black high school girl, Claudette Colvin, refused to give up her seat to a white passenger. She was arrested, handcuffed, and carted off to jail. Martin was asked to serve on a committee to protest to the police commissioner and local bus company manager. The committee received some vague promises, which were not kept. The girl was convicted in court and given a suspended sentence.

The incident stirred Martin's recollection of his own

humiliation as a high school student forced to stand and give up his seat to a white passenger. Indignant, he joined the Montgomery branch of the NAACP and was soon elected to its executive committee. Martin determined to use his eloquence, his influence as a pastor, and his dedication to nonviolence to work for change in the South.

The Jim Crow bus ordinance came to the fore once more on December 1, 1955, when Mrs. Rosa Parks, an NAACP member, boarded a bus after a long day of tiring work. The bus was crowded and she took a seat at the front part of the black section. When more whites boarded, the driver ordered her to give her seat to a white man. Mrs. Parks refused.

"I was just plain tired," she said later, "and my feet hurt."

The driver called a policeman, who arrested her and took her to jail. She was bailed out by a black civil rights activist. The news swept around the black community of Montgomery, arousing a furor. Enough was enough!

Martin offered his Dexter Avenue church for a protest meeting. With leaders of the black community in attendance, all present voted to organize a boycott of the bus lines. Martin was asked to lead the boycott, putting him in a precarious position. But he remembered Thoreau's injunction: "We can no longer lend our cooperation to an evil system."

"When the history books are written in the future," he told his congregation, "somebody will have to say, 'There lived a race of people, of black people, of people who had the moral courage to stand up for their rights.' . . . And we're gonna do that!"

He later reflected, "That was the day that we started a bus protest which electrified the nation."

By the fifth of December the buses of Montgomery began rolling empty of the eighteen thousand blacks who had ridden

...m daily. The city's whites were flabbergasted. There had never been a black boycott in the South before. Downtown businessmen, appalled at the resulting lack of Christmas sales, were distinctly unhappy.

Martin was elected president of a Montgomery Improvement Association to develop the boycott. On the day the boycott began, another mass meeting was called at Martin's church. The pews were packed. Outside four thousand more blacks jammed the streets to hear his message.

"You know, my friends," Martin cried in his rich baritone, "there comes a time when people get tired of being trampled over by the iron feet of oppression!" An explosion of cheers and applause shook the church before he could continue.

"We have no alternative but protest!" Martin thundered. "We have been amazingly patient. . . . But in our protest there will be no cross-burnings, no white person will be taken from his home by a hooded Negro mob and brutally murdered. . . . We will be guided by the highest principles of law and order!"

A fresh roar of acclaim clearly established twenty-six-year-old Martin as leader of the black cause in Montgomery. TV crews began covering the boycott. Contributions and support for the movement flooded in from all over the nation, even from Japan and Switzerland. But anonymous phone callers threatened his life.

"If one day you find me sprawled and dead," Martin told one mass meeting, "I do not want you to retaliate with a single act of violence. I urge you to continue protesting with the same dignity and discipline you have shown so far."

Montgomery police arrested him and put him in jail on a trumped-up traffic charge. Never before behind bars, Martin was shaken but resolved to persist in the boycott, come what

With the end of the Montgomery bus boycott, Rosa Parks takes a front seat in a city bus. The boycott lasted for more than a year, and catapulted the twenty-six-year-old Martin Luther King, Jr., to national prominence. *(UPI/Bettmann)*

may. This first arrest was to be followed by another 120 arrests before his campaign of nonviolent civil disobedience would come to an end, along with his life.

FOUR

RALPH ABERNATHY gathered a large crowd of indignant black pastors, preachers, and deacons outside the police station. Their protests unnerved the warden of the jail. Martin was hustled out of his jail and released on his own recognizance.

The phone threats increased. On January 30, 1956, a bomb was tossed on Martin's front porch. Fortunately, none of his family were hurt by the explosion. A furious black crowd gathered, brandishing weapons. Martin pleaded for calm and peace. More, he even asked his would-be avengers to "love your enemies."

"I want young men and young women who are not alive today but who will come into this world," he told his supporters, "to know that these new privileges and opportunities did not come without somebody suffering and sacrificing for them."

The mayor and police commissioner grew alarmed at the angry gathering of armed blacks. Fearful of a race riot, they posted police at the scene. The whites were relieved when the crowd reluctantly obeyed Martin and returned to their homes.

One white policeman admitted, "If it hadn't been for that nigger preacher, we'd all be dead."

A church member smuggled a pistol into Martin's house for the defense of his family. But as soon as Martin learned about it, he got rid of the gun. "He who lives by the sword," he reminded the militant church member, "will die by it."

In March an all-white Montgomery County jury found Martin and eighty-nine other boycott leaders guilty of violating a thirty-five-year-old statute prohibiting "interference with a business." Martin was sentenced to a fine of $500 or 386 days at hard labor. But in May a federal court ruled bus segregation unconstitutional, nullifying his conviction. City attorneys immediately appealed to the Supreme Court. Meanwhile, the bus boycott persisted.

By this time the White Citizens Councils had enlisted 250,000 members throughout the South. At meetings in Montgomery, teenage whites distributed leaflets reading:

> When in the course of human events it becomes necessary to abolish the Negro race, proper methods should be used. Among these are guns, bows and arrows, sling shots and knives. We hold these truths to be self-evident, that all whites are created equal with certain rights, among these are life, liberty and the pursuit of dead niggers. . . . If we don't stop helping these African flesh eaters, we will soon wake up and find Reverend King in the White House.

Black leaders and some prominent northern white liberals from all over America came to Martin's side to support him in his struggle. Now in great demand around the country to speak on civil rights, Martin contributed fees paid him to the boycott movement. His prestige grew so rapidly that he was called the first black hero the nation had had since Frederick Douglass.

The incensed bus lines tried to sue Martin for $15,000 in damages. But in December their suit was thrown out when the Supreme Court affirmed the lower court's ruling that bus segregation was unconstitutional and therefore illegal.

"It wasn't really a victory for fifteen million Negroes in America," Martin declared. "It was a victory for justice in America."

The Ku Klux Klan desperately sought to nullify the court's decision by spreading terror among Montgomery's blacks. Their racists in white robes drove through the black neighborhood in fifty carloads. They were astonished when black homes remained fully lighted, while blacks strolling the streets viewed the hooded bigots with amused contempt. Martin's victory in the Supreme Court had filled Montgomery's blacks with new confidence and courage. It was the first time American blacks had ever successfully defied the KKK.

When Montgomery's mayor agreed to respect the court's decision, Martin terminated the boycott. He, Ralph Abernathy, and Rosa Parks mounted the first desegregated bus, sitting down in the front seats. The driver said with exaggerated politeness, "We are glad to have you with us this morning, Dr. King."

But one white passenger stood up in the aisle, shouting, "I would rather die and go to hell than sit behind a nigger!"

The battle was not yet won. When the rank-and-file of the boycott attempted to integrate the buses, twenty-two were arrested. Not for another two years were such arrests declared wholly illegal by the Supreme Court. Buses ridden by blacks in front seats were also stoned and fired upon. Some blacks were dragged off and beaten. Ralph Abernathy's house and church were blown up with dynamite, along with three other black churches.

Speaking at a mass meeting in January 1957, Martin pleaded with his followers to respond to this continued violence with nonviolence and love for the perpetrators.

"Oh, Lord," he prayed, "I hope no one will have to die as

a result of our struggle for freedom in Montgomery. Certainly I don't want to die. But if anyone has to die, let it be me!"

"No! No!" screamed his parishioners.

After more bombs exploded and dynamite was found on Martin's porch, Montgomery's white leaders finally felt compelled to take a stand against the violence, and it ceased.

Meanwhile, the bus boycott spread to other cities in the South. This added to the turmoil caused by attempts to desegregate southern schools. Segregationists were infuriated.

"All the people of the South are in favor of segregation," Mississippi Senator James Eastland roared, "and Supreme Court or no Supreme Court we are going to maintain segregation down in Dixie!"

Eleven southern states signed the Southern Manifesto, a document attacking the Court's decisions and pledging resistance.

Martin determined to oppose the manifesto by extending a defiant civil rights campaign all through the South. He called a conference of black leaders in New Orleans to map out strategy. With Ralph Abernathy at his side, he organized the Southern Christian Leadership Conference (SCLC), to which he was promptly elected president. He resigned his pastorate in order to throw all his energies into his new undertaking.

Martin then requested a White House conference on civil rights. Lacking one, he hinted, the SCLC might feel compelled to lead a huge "Prayer Pilgrimage" to Washington. When no response was forthcoming, he prepared plans for this pilgrimage and made sure the press played up the story.

He was so successful in this endeavor that *Time* magazine

put Martin's face on its cover in the February 18, 1957, issue. Martin was described as "the scholarly Negro Baptist minister who in little more than a year had risen from nowhere to become one of the nation's remarkable leaders of men."

Martin set in motion plans for peaceful civil rights demonstrations throughout the South. His father expressed pride in his accomplishments, but opposed Martin's policy of social protest demonstrations. Fearing the danger Martin was incurring by open defiance of the southern white power structure, Martin, Sr., vainly urged his son to return to the safety of the pulpit.

Martin's swift rise to prominence as a black leader determined to challenge Jim Crow laws aroused the hostility of FBI chief J. Edgar Hoover, the racist who had targeted Marcus Garvey for prosecution. Hoover now ordered Martin placed under secret surveillance as a "Communist." Hoover based his conviction on writings by Robert Welch, leader of the extremist right-wing John Birch Society. Welch had "revealed" a secret Red plot for an "independent Negro-Soviet Republic to be carved out of the United States" and predicted "thousands of white citizens will be murdered in the South." Hoover swallowed this nonsense whole.

In 1956 Hoover initiated a program called COINTELPRO. Its operations included infiltration of suspect civil rights and liberal groups, disruption of their activities, and propaganda designed to destroy their credibility. One of Hoover's objectives was to prevent the rise of a "black messiah" who could "unify and electrify a coalition of militant black nationalist groups."

There was no doubt his target was Martin Luther King, Jr.

F I V E

In March 1957 Kwame Nkrumah, the new president of Ghana who had been a great admirer of Marcus Garvey's, invited Martin and black leaders Ralph Bunche, Adam Clayton Powell, A. Philip Randolph, and Roy Wilkins to celebrate Ghana's Independence Day ceremonies. It was the first trip abroad for Martin and Coretta. What impressed Martin most was that Nkrumah had won independence from Britain nonviolently.

Returning home, Martin led his Prayer Pilgrimage to Washington in the summer of 1957. Attended by twenty thousand followers, it was a rehearsal for the great historic march and rally that would follow six years later. In Martin's speech he deplored the "silent and apathetic behavior" of the White House in dealing with race relations. He denounced the failure of the federal government to enforce the right of blacks to vote in the South.

"Give us the ballot," he cried, "and we will no longer have to worry the federal government about our basic rights!"

Yet the White House was reluctant to move forward on civil rights for fear of offending white southern voters. When Martin and Ralph Abernathy met with Vice President Richard Nixon and Secretary of Labor James Mitchell, Nixon simply fended Martin off with vague promises.

But Martin and the SCLC kept the pressure on for enforcement of southern black enfranchisement. In February 1958 Martin announced a Crusade for Citizenship, calling for mass meetings in twenty-one southern cities.

"We want freedom *now*," he cried. "We do not want freedom fed to us in teaspoons over another hundred and fifty years!"

Martin's personal crusade in the South for black civil rights led to more arrests and beatings. He wrote of his struggle in his first book, *Stride Toward Freedom*, published in September 1958. Touring to promote the book, Martin was met by crowds who flocked in to talk to the now-famous author and buy his book. But when he was signing books in a Harlem department store, a demented black woman suddenly stabbed him in the chest with a letter opener. When the news flashed around the nation, tens of thousands prayed for Martin's survival.

After Martin's recovery from an operation, his first words expressed concern for his crazed attacker. "This person needs help," he whispered. "She is not responsible for the violence she has done me. Don't do anything to her; don't prosecute her. Get her healed." The woman was committed to a hospital for the criminally insane.

Ordered by his doctors to take it easy for a while, Martin made a personal pilgrimage to India with Coretta to study Gandhi's revolution. Prime Minister Jawaharlal Nehru invited them to dinner, and Martin gave some speeches at Indian universities.

He also spoke with some Indians who had known Gandhi. Martin was awed when he learned that Gandhi had once told visiting blacks that it might be through American blacks that the message of nonviolent resistance would be heard in the world. He also learned about *Satyagraha*—soul force—the only weapon of Gandhi's nonviolent army. It was with *Satyagraha* that the Mahatma had won his revolution against British oppression.

"I left India more convinced than ever before," Martin related, "that nonviolent resistance is the most potent weapon available to oppressed people in their struggle for freedom. It was a marvelous thing to see the results of a nonviolent campaign." India also left him with a great desire to live as simply as possible, in imitation of Gandhi's leadership.

Martin returned home to more news of southern violence against blacks. Less than a month after he left India, another young black Mississippian, Mack Parker, was lynched by a white mob. As in the case of Emmett Till four years earlier, his murderers went unpunished. The war on blacks in the South continued to escalate, frightening millions of blacks away from the polls.

Segregation continued unabated. Six years after the Supreme Court had ordered all school boards to end segregated education "with all deliberate speed," only 4 percent of black students in the South had succeeded in winning admission to white schools. And white parents in many integrated schools had withdrawn their children, sending them instead to hastily organized all-white private schools.

With the presidential election of 1960 approaching, neither Congress nor the White House was willing to enforce black civil rights and antagonize southern segregationists. As Senator William Fulbright of Arkansas, a respected southern liberal, admitted, "I can't vote my own convictions on civil rights. If I did, I wouldn't be returned to the Senate."

S I X

THE slow progress of the NAACP in winning legal civil rights actions, and the SCLC's failure to win any important new battles since the Montgomery bus boycott, made many college students impatient. A younger generation of activists spearheaded two organizations that would quickly take the lead in the fight for black civil rights.

In 1960 several hundred middle-class black college student leaders organized the Student Nonviolent Coordinating Committee (SNCC, pronounced *snick*). It was founded at a meeting sponsored by Martin's SCLC, which also financed SNCC.

Early that year, SNCC launched its first sit-in protest demonstration in Greensboro, North Carolina. Refused service, four black college students remained seated at a segregated Woolworth's lunch counter until closing time. They returned the next day with sixteen more black students, who also demanded service. By the end of the week hundreds of SNCC students were sitting-in at both Woolworth's and the S. H. Kress store.

The civil rights movement shifted into high gear when SNCC spread sit-ins to a hundred southern cities, involving fifty thousand students in nonviolent demonstrations. Between 1960 and 1963 police arrested, often brutally, over twenty-four thousand demonstrators. Assault and imprisonment were accepted by the energetic volunteers as part of their crusade. As activist Julian Bond described SNCC meetings, "The exchanges would go something like this: 'I was arrested four times in the last thirty days, how about you?' . . . 'Well, I haven't been arrested, but I've been beaten up twice.' "

James Farmer's Congress of Racial Equality (CORE), which included white liberal northern college students, also staged defiant sit-ins and street demonstrations and endured racist brutality. CORE, which had pioneered the sit-in in 1943, joined SNCC in seeking the desegregation of lunch counters, railroad and bus terminals, washrooms, drinking fountains, hotels, parks, beaches, and theaters—in effect, tearing down the public barriers between the races.

It was a tribute to Martin that in both organizations even the young black radicals pledged to respect his philosophy of nonviolence. Many carried signs at their sit-ins reading REMEMBER THE TEACHINGS OF GANDHI AND MARTIN LUTHER KING. When taken off to jail, they joined in singing "We Shall Overcome," which rapidly became the civil rights anthem.

Although the demonstrators were peaceful, they often met with violence. Brutal sheriffs and policemen clubbed them with nightsticks, unleashed attack dogs on them, or blasted them with high-power fire hoses. In Jacksonville, Florida, one demonstrator was killed and seventy people were injured during a three-day riot instigated by Klansmen. At a sit-in in Houston, one black was stabbed and another flogged with a chain by three Klansmen who carved the initials KKK on his chest.

Along with their own courage and determination, the young members of SNCC and CORE had two important assets. In going to jail, they knew the NAACP Legal Defense and Education Fund stood ready to defend them. In staging mass demonstrations, they counted on television cameras to bring their actions to national attention. Watching the demonstrations on TV, thousands of northern white college students were galvanized into joining SNCC and CORE. Millions more northerners, appalled by the violence against peaceful blacks, demanded that the government take action.

While Martin participated in many SNCC and CORE demonstrations, he also kept up his demands for action from Washington. After he threatened to picket the 1960 Democratic Convention in Los Angeles, the Democratic Congress finally felt compelled to pass the Civil Rights Act of 1960. It provided for federal voting referees in all states that barred blacks from voting by one subterfuge or another. It also set off another wave of violent intimidation by segregationists enraged by what they called a federal assault on states' rights. The violence against demonstrators was stepped up, and black churches, schools, and homes were bombed and burned.

The state of Alabama, still furious at Martin for his Montgomery bus boycott, responded with a direct attempt to demolish him as the nation's recognized black leader. Using the same kind of government harassment that brought down Marcus Garvey, the state spuriously charged Martin with falsifying his income tax returns. But the effort fell flat when even an all-white southern jury felt compelled to acquit him.

One month before election day, Martin was arrested on a pretext by the sheriff of De Kalb County, tried, and sentenced to six months of hard labor. SCLC appealed to Vice President Nixon to intercede for him. But as the Republican candidate to succeed Eisenhower, Nixon declined for fear of losing southern white votes. Instead Democratic opponent John Kennedy phoned Coretta to ask if there was anything he could do to help. Shortly afterward his brother, Robert, phoned the judge in the case and persuaded him to release Martin from jail on bail pending an appeal.

Martin's father had planned to vote for Nixon, but now he shouted to his congregation, "If I had a suitcase full of votes, I'd take them all and place them at Senator Kennedy's feet!"

The news quickly flashed around the South. When John F. Kennedy won a narrow presidential victory over Nixon, Martin and other black leaders declared that the black vote had made the difference. Martin then attempted to spur Kennedy into taking action on civil rights by writing an article for *The Nation*. "The new administration," he wrote, "has the opportunity to be the first in one hundred years of American history to adopt a radically new approach to the question of civil rights. . . . The day is past for tolerating vicious and inhuman opposition on a subject which determines the lives of 22 million Americans."

Kennedy refused to admit any obligation to the black community for fear of alienating the southern Democrats in Congress. To keep their support, he appointed three notorious segregationists to federal judgeships in the South.

But Kennedy also inspired liberal young Americans with the idealistic cry, "Ask not what your country can do for you—ask what you can do for your country!" Many northern white college students met this challenge by volunteering for the Freedom Rides, SNCC's and CORE's next major assault on segregation.

S E V E N

THE Freedom Rides were a joint project of SNCC, CORE, and the SCLC, intended to desegregate southern interstate buses and terminals. Martin was named chairman of the coordinating committee, and James Farmer, the head of CORE, directed the Freedom Riders.

On May 4, 1961, two integrated buses left Washington for the South. At each stop, Freedom Riders dismounted and desegregated the lunch counters and restrooms. At first their reception was hostile but not violent. But when they reached Rock Hill, South Carolina, they were savagely beaten by racists before police finally intervened.

When the first bus arrived at Anniston, Alabama, a waiting mob beat the riders, firebombed the bus, and smashed its windows. Later the second bus reached the Montgomery terminal, where the Klan had assembled thousands of infuriated racists armed with metal pipes, baseball bats, and other

The Freedom Riders faced danger again and again. ABOVE, a bus smokes after being firebombed by a crowd of some 200 angry whites in Anniston, Alabama. *(The Bettmann Archive)* BELOW, two young Freedom Riders clean up after a brutal beating in Montgomery, Alabama. *(UPI/Bettmann)*

weapons. Although CORE had notified Montgomery police in advance, no officer was in sight. But NBC-TV and *Life* photographers were on hand to record what happened when the bus doors opened.

As soon as the Freedom Riders dismounted, they were seized and thrown over a rail to a cement parking lot ten feet below, then pursued and clubbed, punched, or thrown to the ground. Rioters hurled themselves at the newsmen, smashing their equipment. John Seigenthaler, an aide to Attorney General Robert Kennedy sent along as an observer, was knocked unconscious. Twenty-two Freedom Riders were injured.

The riot raged for over twenty minutes before police arrived. They made no effort to render first aid to the injured and only pretended to call for ambulances. When asked why an ambulance failed to show up, Montgomery Public Safety Commissioner L. B. Sullivan shrugged and said, "It was broken down and could not come."

FBI agents present simply stood by and took notes. A strong supporter of segregation and the White Citizens Councils, FBI chief J. Edgar Hoover had instructed his men to expect violence *from* blacks, not *against* them.

Martin rushed to Montgomery the following morning. A furious Robert Kennedy dispatched seven hundred U.S. marshals and hundreds of National Guardsmen to protect the Freedom Riders. Alabama Governor John Patterson angrily accused President Kennedy of "interfering in the state to protect outside agitators" and blamed the Freedom Riders for the riot.

Ralph Abernathy's First Baptist Church was jammed to hear Martin address a rally. Several thousand whites surrounded the church, many shouting for it to be burned. Inside, people screamed as rocks and bottles crashed through the stained-glass windows. When the rioters began burning cars, Martin phoned Robert Kennedy asking for more U.S. marshals, since those present seemed to be fraternizing with the mob and the police.

"The law may not be able to make a man love me," Martin cried to his followers, "but it can keep him from lynching me!"

With Ralph Abernathy, he emerged from the front door to plead with the mob to let those in the church go home in peace. A tear-gas bomb hurled at his head forced him back inside. Martin led the people imprisoned in the church in prayer and choruses of "We Shall Overcome" until they were able to leave at dawn.

Martin and Governor Patterson blamed each other for the violence. "The best thing for King to do," Patterson snapped, "is to get out of Alabama as quickly as he can, because he's a menace to the people of this city."

Martin and Ralph Abernathy next went to Albany, Georgia, after receiving a call for help from Freedom Riders who had been jailed in December 1961. At a mass rally in a local church, Martin pleaded with his supporters, "Don't stop now! Keep moving. Don't get weary, children. We will wear them down by our capacity to suffer!"

The next afternoon he led a protest procession of 257 blacks singing "We Shall Overcome" to city hall. They were stopped by Police Chief Laurie Pritchett and more than one hundred police officers. Ordered to disperse the crowd, Martin refused. He and the demonstrators were arrested, increasing the number of imprisoned blacks in and around Albany to more than seven hundred.

After four days the town called a truce. Martin and the others in jail were released on bail, subject to further prosecution. "As long as King stayed in jail," Pritchett said with a sigh, "we would have problems."

Albany now agreed not to prevent the integration of terminal facilities—a hollow victory, since this had already been ordered by the Interstate Commerce Commission, under pressure from Robert Kennedy. Albany still refused to budge on Martin's demand that it also integrate its buses, parks, libraries, and theaters and hire some black officers.

Incensed, Martin attempted to organize another mass protest. But Albany won a federal injunction blocking it. When Martin phoned Robert Kennedy for help, the attorney general now only hemmed and hawed. He told Martin it might be wise to "close up" activities in Albany at this time.

Martin consented reluctantly, not wanting to alienate the Kennedy administration, which SNCC now relied upon for enforcement of the civil rights laws. Other black leaders criticized Martin for backing down in Albany, and also for letting himself be bailed out of jail.

"I'm sorry I was bailed out," Martin later explained. "I didn't understand at the time what was happening. We thought the victory had been won. When we got out, we discovered it was all a hoax."

The *New York Herald Tribune* called the Albany campaign "one of the most stunning defeats of his career."

E I G H T

MARTIN now made the bold decision to attack southern racism in its most prominent fortress. Birmingham, Alabama, placed under martial law by Governor Patterson, was ruled by the notorious Commissioner of Public Safety Eugene "Bull" Connor, who terrorized blacks with his brutal police force.

"It is the most thoroughly segregated city in America," Martin told SNCC. "All the evils and injustices the Negro can be subjected to are right there in Birmingham."

But before taking on Birmingham, Martin and Ralph Abernathy returned to Albany, Georgia, to stand trial for disorderly conduct and parading without a permit. Sentenced to pay a fine or spend forty-five days at hard labor, they chose jail. Albany blacks began to organize new demonstrations, and Washington put pressure on Albany's mayor. After spending two days in jail, Martin and Ralph were set free on the pretext that someone had paid their fines.

Martin was determined not to repeat the mistakes of Albany in Birmingham. He had come under criticism from black civil rights activists who complained that his nonviolent policies were too tame to defeat southern racism. Radical black groups were starting to demand armed revolution. Even the students of SNCC and CORE were becoming impatient with the lack of real progress.

Visiting the White House, Martin told the president that blacks were on the verge of exploding against southern racism and needed a strong new civil rights program to support them. Kennedy replied evasively that Martin should solve race problems by simply registering more southern black voters.

Martin demanded to know whether Attorney General Robert Kennedy was prepared to protect the demonstrations he was planning for Birmingham if the city's officials reacted with violence. If his people suffered broken heads, Martin made it clear, he would call publicly for government intervention. But Robert Kennedy had no taste for a confrontation with his powerful FBI chief, J. Edgar Hoover, who still insisted that Martin and the SCLC were dangerous "Communist conspirators."

Despite the lack of federal support, Martin, Ralph, and aide Andrew Young launched their crusade in March 1963. On the first day of demonstrations, thirty blacks were arrested for attempting to integrate downtown lunch counters. Speaking to a prayer rally that evening, Martin cried, "We are heading for freedom land, and nothing is going to stop us. We are going to make Birmingham the center of antidiscrimination activity in the nation. I have come here to stay until something is done."

Martin ordered a black boycott of all Birmingham stores until they were desegregated, a blow that greatly upset the city's businesspeople. Supported by the SCLC, SNCC, CORE, and local black groups, he also staged daily demonstration marches. All were broken up, with demonstrators carted off to jail singing freedom songs. Thousands of blacks cheered them from the sidewalks while TV news cameras recorded their arrests. In the first week five hundred were arrested, with three hundred refusing to pay fines or be bailed out.

An Alabama state court issued an injunction to halt Martin's demonstrations. He defied the injunction by announcing he would lead a march through the center of Birmingham.

"I've decided to go to jail," he told his followers. "I don't know what's going to happen. . . . If enough people are willing to go jail, I believe it will force the city officials to act, or force the federal government to act."

Nearly a thousand spectators watched Martin lead fifty volunteers toward waiting police lines commanded by Bull Connor.

"Freedom has come to Birmingham!" cried one onlooker.

Martin and Ralph were promptly arrested and thrown in solitary confinement. All the marchers were jailed. The SCLC was out of bail money. And there was no sign of outrage from

Washington. Robert Kennedy maintained that the marches were "ill-timed" and told reporters, "The federal government has no authority to take legal action or to intervene in Birmingham as the situation now stands."

Alone in his dark, unlit cell, Martin wondered if Bull Connor would have him beaten by his jailers or killed, explaining that Martin had "tried to escape." This time he felt alone and discouraged.

When SCLC attorneys asked to see Martin, permission was denied. Coretta, frantic with worry, tried to reach the president. He phoned back to assure her that he had sent the FBI into Birmingham to check on Martin, who was reported safe so far.

"Of course," John F. Kennedy said with a sigh, "Birmingham is a very difficult place." Awareness of the president's surveillance, however, abruptly brought privileges to Martin in jail. He was allowed to exercise, take a shower, have a mattress and pillow, and phone his relieved wife.

Eight leading white Birmingham churchmen issued a public statement denouncing the "unwise and untimely" actions of an "outside agitator." They called upon Martin and his supporters to cease their challenge, insisting that "a cause should be pressed in the courts and in negotiations among local leaders, not in the streets."

Martin replied in a historic and eloquent open letter to them written in the margins of newspapers and on toilet paper.

I am in Birmingham because injustice is here. . . . Injustice anywhere is a threat to justice everywhere. . . . It is unfortunate that demonstrations are taking place in Birmingham, but it is even more

unfortunate that the city's white power structure left
the Negro community with no alternative. . . . Birmingham's ugly record of brutality is widely
known. . . . There have been more unsolved bombings
of Negro homes and churches in Birmingham than in
any other city in the nation.

And he took white "moderates" to task for putting order above
justice.

Famous singer Harry Belafonte, one of Martin's supporters, raised $50,000 to bail 166 blacks out of jail. Martin asked
to remain with the roughly 250 other blacks still imprisoned,
but the SCLC insisted that he must come out to plan the next
move of the campaign. Reluctantly, after eight days in jail,
Martin emerged from his thirteenth incarceration.

Speaking to his followers before TV cameras, Martin
moved some white spectators to tears when he cautioned,
"We must not lose faith in our white brothers."

On May 2, 1963, Martin addressed children at the Sixteenth Street Baptist Church. Inspired by his eloquence, they
marched downtown singing. Almost a thousand youngsters
were arrested, overflowing all the jails in the city and county.

"This is the first time in the history of our struggle,"
Martin told his followers, "that we have been able, literally,
to fill the jails. . . . This is the fulfillment of a dream, for I
have always felt that if we could fill the jails . . . it would be
a magnificent expression of the determination of the Negro,
and a marvelous way to lay the whole issue before the conscience of the community and the nation."

The conscience of the nation was indeed troubled by the
spectacle of police chasing and brutally handling black children seen on TV newscasts. But that didn't stop Bull Connor

from ordering his police to repeat the violence against the next day's marchers.

On the third day Connor was determined to teach the "niggers" a real lesson. He organized barricades guarded by police with attack dogs and nightsticks at the ready. Fire engines stood by with high-pressure hoses connected to hydrants, while a light tank patrolled the streets.

As thousands of children, teenagers, and mothers marched toward the barricades, Connor roared, "Turn those hoses on!"

Powerful streams of water struck women and children, knocking them flat. A few were sent spinning across sidewalks as the torrents blasted them mercilessly. Some marchers were lifted bodily by the pressure of the streams and hurled against buildings. The pressure was so deadly that it stripped off clothing, ripped bark off the trees, and tore bricks out of walls.

Connor next unleashed the police dogs, which attacked the children savagely. Police beat demonstrators with clubs and shocked them with cattle prods, even when some kneeled to pray. One woman was pinioned on the sidewalk with a cop's knee on her throat.

March leaders pleaded with blacks to remain nonviolent.

"We want to redeem the souls of people like Bull Connor!" one shouted through a bullhorn.

Almost twenty-five hundred demonstrators were arrested and jailed. More than fifty were severely injured. If previous scenes of violence by Birmingham police had shocked TV viewers, these new scenes evoked a tremendous outcry for federal action against southern racism.

As Martin had predicted, "TV is going to be the medium in which we bring this country face-to-face with itself." Protests flooded the White House and Congress. Newspaper editorials demanded that the persecution of southern blacks be stopped at once.

"Connor became an international symbol," *Time* noted, "of blind, cruel Southern racism." Connor's ruthless brutality had accomplished in fifteen vicious minutes what Martin's exhortations had failed to do in fifteen years.

Martin challenged Connor, "We will meet your physical force with soul force. . . . We will meet your capacity to inflict suffering with our capacity to endure suffering."

As the next church group prepared to march, Martin told them, "Don't ever be afraid to die. . . . No man is free if he fears death. . . . You must say, somehow, 'I don't have much money, I don't have much education, I may not be able to read and write, but I have the capacity to die!' "

The congregation set out on another defiant march. When they reached Connor's barricade, he furiously ordered them to disperse. The black minister leading the march replied calmly, "We will stand here till we die."

Blacks behind him dropped to their knees and prayed.

"Turn those hoses on, dammit!" Connor howled.

But this time shamefaced firemen refused to attack the marchers, who moved through the silent ranks of firemen and police.

The marchers reached a park, prayed, then marched back to their church singing "Ain't Gonna Let Nobody Turn Me 'Round." For Martin, it was a victory of pure moral force.

But his jubilation over the completed march was short-lived. While mostly middle-class blacks had participated in the protests, Birmingham's jobless, poor, and uneducated blacks had sat on the sidelines. For two weeks they had grown increasingly furious watching other blacks, including children, ruthlessly assaulted. The last straws were two time bombs that destroyed the home of Martin's brother, A. D. King, and the dynamiting of a motel that seriously injured several blacks.

Their rage finally exploded. Rampaging from the Birmingham ghetto, they attacked police with rocks, bottles, and knives. White-owned shops and cars were set on fire. Police arrested fifty of the rioters, beating them severely.

Martin was appalled. But the outbreak marked the entry of previously intimidated poor blacks into the protest movement. It was also a vivid demonstration of how suppressed black anger at white oppression could flare into violence.

Phoning the White House, Martin urged that since the state of Alabama refused to put limits on itself, federal limits needed to be imposed. The violence in Birmingham forced President Kennedy, finally, to take a firm stand on civil rights, regardless of what it might cost him in the lost support of southern congressmen.

"Fires of frustration," Kennedy declared, "are burning in every city, North and South, where legal remedies are not at hand."

He announced that the following week he would ask Congress for a strong civil rights bill. Martin was invited to the White House for a conference on drafting the new bill.

"Bull Connor has done as much for civil rights," John F. Kennedy told Martin with a smile, "as Abraham Lincoln!"

N I N E

DESPITE Martin's victories in Birmingham, the war on blacks continued in Mississippi, which Roy Wilkins, executive director of the NAACP, designated as "the worst American state." After Martin left Birmingham, the board of education expelled one thousand black children from school as a penalty for participating in the civil rights marches. Eight

SNCC leaders were arrested and tortured in Greenwood. But the worst blow came in June 1963, when Medgar Evers, leader of the Mississippi NAACP and Martin's good friend, was shot dead in his doorway by a white racist. After the assassin was acquitted by an all-white jury, Evers's wife said she had wished for a machine gun to mow down every white in sight.

Martin was now anxious to put pressure on Congress to pass the president's new civil rights bill. A. Philip Randolph suggested a demonstration he had dreamed of for twenty years—a huge, dignified march of blacks on Washington to demand jobs and freedom. Martin's eyes sparkled. His one-time assistant, Bayard Rustin, was assigned to coordinate the march. The NAACP, SCLC, SNCC, CORE, and Urban League were all persuaded to take part.

Martin left on a national tour to win support for the march and to encourage other black city crusades like Birmingham's.

Now acknowledged as the most effective spokesman for his race, Martin received acclaim in city after city. In Los Angeles thousands of listeners roared in delight when he quoted an old ex-slave to express what many Alabama blacks were now feeling: " 'We ain't what we ought to be and we ain't what we want to be and we ain't what we're going to be. But thank God we ain't what we was!' "

In Detroit Martin led 125,000 people in what he called a Freedom Walk. He cried out to huge crowds, "I submit to you that if a man hasn't discovered something he will die for, he ain't fit to live!" Listeners rose to give him a standing ovation.

Martin was shocked and disappointed when President Kennedy told him and other black leaders that the White

House opposed the impending Washington march. Fearing an angry congressional backlash, Kennedy called it "ill-timed."

"Frankly," Martin replied wryly, "I have never engaged in any direct action movement which did not seem ill-timed." Then, looking squarely at Robert Kennedy, he added, "Some people thought Birmingham ill-timed."

JFK was worried less about Martin's nonviolent contingents in the march than about black radicals. He suspected them of wanting to bring the whole government to a halt. To add to his doubts, FBI chief J. Edgar Hoover warned the White House that Martin's march was "Communist-inspired."

But Robert Kennedy urged his brother to show support for the march, fearing the impact of Martin's continued public criticism of the Kennedy administration. The president then invited Martin and the other black leaders to the White House after the march for a "camp meeting" to promote racial understanding.

An estimated 250,000 people, about a third of them white, participated in the march on Washington on August 28, 1963. Many celebrities made appearances, including Burt Lancaster, Marlon Brando, Sidney Poitier, Harry Belafonte, Joan Baez, Odetta, Mahalia Jackson, and Lena Horne. All the major TV networks and international TV crews covered the event extensively. Local bands made the occasion melodious, as did the demonstrators, who sang "We Shall Overcome" as they marched from the Washington Monument to the Lincoln Memorial.

Speakers addressed the crowd from the steps of the Lincoln Memorial. Martin was saved for last. When Randolph introduced him as "the moral leader of the nation," a storm of cheers and applause erupted.

Martin Luther King, Jr., waves to the crowd during the March on Washington. An estimated 250,000 people turned out for the march, making it at that time the largest human rights demonstration in the history of America. *(UPI/Bettmann Newsphotos)*

"I have a dream," Martin cried in his rich, ringing
baritone:

> that one day on the red hills of Georgia the sons of
> former slaves and the sons of former slaveowners will
> be able to sit down together at the table of brother-
> hood. I have a dream that one day even the state of
> Mississippi, a state sweltering with people's injus-
> tices, with the heat of oppression, will be transformed
> into an oasis of freedom and justice. I have a dream
> that my four little children will one day live in a
> nation where they will be judged not by the color of
> their skin but by the content of their character.

He ended his speech eloquently by hoping that one day
soon freedom would ring out across the country, uniting "all
of God's children" to "join hands and sing in the words of the
old Negro spiritual, 'Free at last! Free at last! Great God Almighty, we are free at last!' "

After a moment of awed silence, 250,000 listeners suddenly went wild, screaming in ecstasy, aware that they had
heard one of the most moving speeches of all time. Marshals
had to surround Martin to save him from the crushing em-
braces of the crowd that surged toward him. Millions of white
viewers watching on TV felt deeply touched as never before
by the black cause so eloquently pleaded by its leading
spokesman.

After the march, Washington's Deputy Chief of Police
Howard Covell admitted of the crowd, "We could not handle
this number if it were not peaceful." But for racist Americans,
this peaceful demonstration was the signal for a fresh series
of violent outrages.

T E N

L E S S than three weeks after the march on Washington, white racists gave their answer to Martin Luther King. A bomb was hurled into the Sixteenth Street Baptist Church in Birmingham during Sunday school, killing four little black girls. Shocked and grieved, Martin returned to Birmingham to console the dead girls' parents. No word of condolence came from Governor George Wallace.

At the funeral service for the dead girls, Martin delivered a service that ended, "The innocent blood of these little girls may well serve as the redemptive force that will bring new light to this dark city."

Heavy-hearted, Martin knew he would now have great difficulty in keeping his struggle nonviolent. Black writer John Killens said grimly, "Negroes must be prepared to protect themselves with guns." Many furious black radicals now endorsed this view. When Martin spoke in Harlem, they made their disagreement with him clear, pelting him with eggs.

On November 22, 1963, Martin was horrified when violence overtook even the president of the United States. Reacting somberly to the news of John F. Kennedy's assassination, he said to Coretta, "This is what is going to happen to me also. I keep telling you, this is a sick society." Publicly he declared, "It is the same climate that murdered Medgar Evers in Mississippi and four innocent children in Birmingham."

The new president, Lyndon B. Johnson, summoned Martin to the White House on December 3 to discuss the new civil rights bill JFK had sent to Congress. At first Martin was skeptical about white southerner Johnson. But the president convinced Martin that he was fully determined to push the bill through Congress, despite opposition by southern Democrats.

Martin appeared again on the cover of *Time* magazine, now as its "Man of the Year." Despite the growing opposition from black radicals, *Time* called him "the unchallenged voice of the Negro people." Martin told the SCLC, "I would like to think that my selection . . . was not a personal tribute, but a tribute to the whole freedom movement."

In May 1964 violence against civil rights workers sent Martin and Ralph Abernathy to St. Augustine, Florida. The Ku Klux Klan there had burned four blacks to death, bombed black homes, and boasted of a hunting club whose members hunted human "coons." Five black and two white civil rights activists had sought to integrate a motel. When they dove into its swimming pool, the manager hurled two jugs of hydrochloric acid into the pool. Other blacks attempting to swim at the public beach were beaten off by a white mob armed with clubs.

Responding to the plea for help from the besieged activists, Martin organized a civil rights march. Police and Klansmen attacked the demonstrators, the police arresting and jailing Martin and Ralph Abernathy. Three days later they were bailed out so that Martin could fly to New Haven to receive an honorary degree from Yale University.

CORE, SNCC, the NAACP, and the SCLC now united in a coalition called the Council of Federated Organizations (COFO). It promptly announced a new Freedom Summer campaign in Mississippi. As Eleanor Holmes Norton of SNCC later explained this decision, "We thought if we brought down Mississippi, the rest of the South would have to fall."

One priority of the campaign would be combatting the lessons taught in state schools, clearly expressed in a third- and fourth-grade textbook provided by the White Citizens Council of Mississippi:

> God wanted the white people to live alone. And He wanted colored people to live alone. . . . White men built America so they could make the rules. . . . Do you know that some people want the Negroes to live with white people? These people want us to be unhappy. . . . Did you know that our country will grow weak if we mix the races?

New Freedom Riders, some eight hundred black and white college students from all over the country, flooded Mississippi. Working with blacks for the first time, many white students discovered their own hidden prejudices, first expressed in their surprise at finding their black counterparts both educated and intelligent. Together the students shared the physical dangers southern blacks faced as they set up "freedom schools," teaching nonviolent protest and helping register black voters.

Governor Paul Johnson, who ridiculed the NAACP as standing for "Niggers, Alligators, Apes, Coons and Possums," called on Mississippians to battle the "invasion" of his state. Enraged segregationists destroyed almost forty black churches. Over the course of Freedom Summer, police beat up eighty civil rights workers and arrested over one thousand. Three were murdered.

In June, soon after the COFO workers arrived, three young volunteers, white New Yorkers Michael Schwerner and Andrew Goodman and black Mississippian James Chaney, were arrested. Released at night, they were then reported missing.

Six weeks later their bodies were found buried in a local dam. This was the first time young white civil rights workers had been slain in the South. Their deaths stunned white America. The Mississippi courts refused to convict seven Klansmen of the murders, but a federal court eventually did so three years later.

Even death was not allowed to interfere with segregation. Mississippi refused to permit black Chaney to be buried beside his white companions.

TV news teams rushed to Mississippi. The events they reported further shocked America. When Martin led a People to People march to protest the violence, the camp where the marchers were spending the night was attacked, the people driven off with tear gas and rifle butts. Regrouping the next day, the marchers were again halted in front of the capitol building in Jackson by a cordon of menacing police. Turning, Martin raised his arm in defiance and addressed his followers.

"One day right here in the state of Mississippi," he cried, "justice will become a reality for all!"

E L E V E N

B Y the end of Freedom Summer, the civil rights movement had achieved some major goals. Thanks to President Johnson's support, JFK's civil rights bill was passed by Congress. The strongest civil rights legislation since southern reconstruction, it required school desegregation "as quickly as possible," forbade the use of different voting requirements for blacks and whites, and made discrimination in public places illegal.

Freedom Riders in Mississippi had also succeeded in registering fifty thousand blacks in the new Mississippi Freedom Democratic party. But segregationists had kept the new voters from the polls. So when the 1964 Democratic

Convention was held in Atlantic City, New Jersey, the Freedom Democrats sent their own all-black delegation to challenge Mississippi's all-white delegates.

Martin insisted that the Freedom Democrats be seated in place of the white delegation, since the latter had forfeited their right to represent their state by violating the new civil rights law. The Democratic credentials committee offered to make the delegation half black, half white. Martin accepted the compromise for the SCLC. But the black delegates refused and walked out. Though they were respectful of Martin, black militants angrily blamed him for not forcing the issue.

In October Martin was astonished by unexpected news from Norway: he had been awarded the Nobel Peace Prize. J. Edgar Hoover, dismayed, vengefully launched a plot to discredit Martin.

Before the march on Washington, Hoover had obtained Robert Kennedy's reluctant permission to tap Martin's phone. He had used the information from the wiretap to plan ugly rumors about Martin with the press. Now a bug in a hotel room Martin used to confer with other civil rights leaders yielded a tape that suggested that Martin had had affairs with women. Hoover mailed one copy anonymously to Coretta, hoping to provoke a scandalous divorce that would ruin Martin.

A month before Martin was scheduled to leave for Oslo to accept the Nobel Peace Prize, Hoover mailed another copy of the tape to Martin himself. The anonymous note accompanying it said, "King, there is only one thing left for you to do. You have just 34 days in which to do it. . . . There is but one way out for you. You better take it before your filthy fraudulent self is bared to the nation." Investigating congressmen later called the note an attempt to drive Martin to suicide.

Undaunted by the vengeful FBI director's scheme, Martin left for Oslo to accept the Nobel Prize. At a ceremony attended by Norway's king and queen, he declared:

> We have learned to fly the air like birds and even swim the sea like fish, but we have not learned the simple arts of living together like brothers. . . . Nonviolence has also meant that my people in the agonizing struggles of recent years have taken suffering upon themselves instead of inflicting it on others. . . . It seeks no victory over anyone. It seeks to liberate American society and to share in the self-liberation of all the people.

Returning home, in early 1965 Martin targeted Selma, Alabama, where the black population exceeded whites but where blacks were kept away from the polls by tough Sheriff Jim Clark and his deputies. Martin got his first taste of Selma's hospitality when he and his aides registered in the Hotel Albert. Suddenly he was attacked, getting smashed twice on the head and kicked hard in the thigh before the racist was seized.

Despite his injuries, Martin led a procession of four hundred blacks to Selma's courthouse to vote. Sheriff Clark snapped, "No registrars working today. Bring them some other time."

Martin led a giant demonstration back to the courthouse on February 1. He, Ralph Abernathy, and 770 demonstrators were promptly arrested. Next day 550 more protesters joined them in jail. Many were schoolchildren who sang "Ain't

Gonna Let Jim Clark Turn Me 'Round" and "I Love Jim Clark in My Heart."

After four days in jail, Martin and Ralph Abernathy were released on bail to revive the demonstrations. When 165 children marched, Clark forced them to trot nearly three miles out of town, shocked by electric cattle prods from the deputies' cars.

"Selma will never get right," Martin told a chapel congregation, "and Dallas County will never get right until we get rid of Jim Clark." Two days later, coincidentally, Clark suffered a mild heart attack. His deputies were dumbfounded when two hundred black youngsters heeded Martin's urging to "love your enemy" by kneeling publicly to pray for Clark's recovery.

While Martin continued his unsuccessful attempts to register blacks at Selma's courthouse, news reached him that militant black activist Malcolm X had been assassinated in Harlem. Martin felt a chill of premonition. In nearby Marion, police had shot and killed a civil rights demonstrator who had tried to keep his mother from being clubbed. Medgar Evers had been assassinated. Goodman, Chaney, and Schwerner had been murdered in Mississippi. Even President Kennedy had been killed.

Martin felt certain he would be next. He had received information that the Ku Klux Klan was trying to hire a hit man to kill him. It was only a matter of time, he reflected sorrowfully.

T W E L V E

IN MARCH Martin took time out from the action in Selma to fly to Washington. He urged President Johnson to expedite a new voting rights bill that would replace county voting registrars with federal registrars. Johnson promised he would if Martin tried to keep black protests peaceful.

Returning to Selma, Martin announced he would now lead a fifty-four-mile demonstration march to Montgomery, Alabama's capital.

"There will be no march!" snapped Governor Wallace.

At the last moment SNCC aides insisted that Martin not lead the march himself, because they had been warned of a plot to kill him in the confusion of a confrontation with police. Reluctantly, Martin let two other SNCC officials lead five hundred blacks and a few white people up the highway toward Montgomery. In a little while they were stopped by Jim Clark, a mounted posse, and the Alabama Highway Patrol.

"If you march," Clark snarled, "you will do so over my dead body!" When the marchers tried to advance, sixty masked police hurled tear gas and charged the marchers' ranks, clubs swinging. Twenty people were knocked down. Demonstrators kneeling to pray were slashed with bullwhips by the mounted police.

"Get those goddam niggers!" Clark yelled. "Get those goddam *white* niggers!" His horsemen chased the fleeing demonstrators with electric cattle prods. Sixteen people had to be hospitalized and another fifty were badly hurt.

TV cameras captured the event, freshly outraging the nation. From all over the country 450 white ministers, priests, rabbis, and nuns came to Selma to join the demonstrations.

Martin immediately planned a new march. A court order barred it, and the president pled with Martin not to lead it.

"We have no alternative but to keep moving with determination," Martin told the three thousand demonstrators who gathered to begin the march. "We've gone too far now to turn back. We cannot afford to stop because Alabama and our nation have a date with destiny. . . . I have got to march. I do not know what lies ahead of us. There may be beatings, jailings, tear gas. But I would rather die on the highways of Alabama than make a butchery of my conscience!"

Led by Martin, Ralph Abernathy, and James Farmer, the demonstrators marched arm in arm, five abreast, until they were stopped by troopers after crossing a bridge. When they were commanded to obey the court injunction and disperse, they knelt to pray. Then, worried that an attempt to pass police barricades could bring death or serious injury to some of his followers, Martin led them back to the church where they had first gathered.

Martin's failure to persevere in the march led to some disillusionment with his leadership in the ranks of SNCC, NAACP, CORE, and even his own SCLC. Militant blacks urged more dynamic action.

That night three white clergymen who had taken part in the demonstration were assaulted by Klansmen. The Reverend James Reeb of Boston was clubbed to death, setting off another wave of national indignation.

CORE's James Farmer angrily demanded that the president warn Governor Wallace to stop sanctioning the persecution of civil rights workers, or face jail. Johnson summoned Wallace to the White House and pleaded, as one southerner to another, "How does history want to remember us?"

Wallace claimed he was unable to protect the civil rights workers. Johnson then federalized the Alabama National Guard and ordered the secretary of defense to send an equal number of federal troops to Alabama to protect the marchers.

On March 15 the president addressed a joint session of Congress to ask for passage of the Voting Rights Act of 1965. He declared:

The real hero of this struggle is the American Negro. His courage to risk safety and even to risk his life, have awakened the conscience of this nation. . . . No laws that we now have on the books . . . can insure the right to vote when local officials are determined to deny it. . . . In such a case our duty must be clear to all of us. . . . There is no issue of states' rights. . . . There is only the struggle for human rights.

The new law was passed, and federal examiners were sent to southern districts to register black voters and arrest anyone who tried to stop them. The act made it possible, during the next two years, for some two hundred black candidates to be elected to office in the South.

Johnson also asked Congress to investigate the Klan, calling them a "hooded society of bigots." A congressional probe revealed that the Klan now had 381 Klaverns (chapters) throughout the South and also in six northern states. Many members belonged to local police forces. All Klan mobs operated under oaths of secrecy enforced by "beatings, bombings and yes, even death," the Congressional report revealed. The Klan was also found to have hatched plans to assassinate President Johnson and blow up the White House.

The Klan once again planned to assassinate Martin when he resumed the Selma-to-Montgomery march, for which Johnson had forced the lifting of the court injunction. But this time federal troops were on hand to protect the marchers.

As Army helicopters whirled overhead, Martin assembled the two thousand marchers. "Walk together, children," he urged. "Don't you get weary, and it will lead us to the Promised Land. And Alabama will be a new Alabama, and America will be a new America."

Over the three days of the march, there was no resistance, and the marcher's ranks had swelled to twenty-five thousand. As Martin, with Coretta at his side, led them into Montgomery for a victory rally, thunderous applause greeted him.

"There were those who said that we would get here only over their dead bodies," he told the rally,

> but all the world together knows that we are here, and that we are standing before the forces of power in the state of Alabama saying: "We Ain't Gonna Let Nobody Turn Us 'Round." . . . The battle is in our hands. . . . I know some of you are asking today, "How long will it take?'. . . How long? Not long, because no lie can live forever. How long? Not long, because you will reap what you sow.

Many of the celebrities who had joined in the march on Washington entertained the crowds at their celebration in Montgomery. Among those present to rejoice, ten years after her own defiance had led to the civil rights struggle, was Rosa Parks.

But the march was not without tragedy. When Viola Liuzzo, a white Detroit mother of five, drove a young black civil rights worker from Selma to Montgomery, she was shot and killed by Klansmen. Outraged, Martin appeared on the TV program *Meet the Press* to ask for a nationwide boycott of all Alabama products, as well as a Treasury withdrawal of all federal funds from Alabama banks.

The first major black riot broke out, not in the South, but in Los Angeles's Watts ghetto five days after the new Voting Rights Act was passed. Mob passions, already running high over allegations of police brutality, were intensified by speakers voicing bitter complaints against black unemployment,

King officially starts the last leg of the 1965 Selma-to-Montgomery march. At King's left is his wife, Coretta Scott King, and at his right are Ralph Bunche and Ralph Abernathy (with umbrella). *(UPI/Bettmann)*

bad schools, high ghetto prices, and grinding poverty. To the cry of "Burn, baby, burn!" white-owned cars were overturned and set ablaze, and white businesses were torched in six days of violent rioting. By the time the riot ended, thirty-four people were dead, four thousand were arrested, and 209 buildings were destroyed.

In an effort to help calm the Watts community, Martin immediately flew to Los Angeles. Conferring with city officials and California Governor Pat Brown, he pointed out that the riot was simply a symptom of the racism that they had long tolerated.

While grateful to President Johnson for all he had done for the black cause, Martin now broke with the president over his foreign policy. "The war in Vietnam must be stopped," he insisted. In keeping with his Nobel Peace Prize, he promised to organize anti–Vietnam War peace rallies and teach-ins. Johnson was furious.

In August Martin marched for the first time in an antiwar demonstration, held in Chicago. Here he was threatened by rioting mobs controlled by prowar Mayor Richard Daley and knocked down by a hurled rock. He also heard a popular song sung by Chicago high school students:

> I wish I were an Alabama trooper,
> That is what I really want to be,
> 'Cause if I were an Alabama trooper,
> I would kill a nigger legally.

"I had to come up north," Martin told the demonstrators wryly, "to learn how to hate."

While Martin continued his efforts for southern blacks, the growing agitation by ghetto blacks drew him increasingly to the North. Martin returned to Chicago in the summer of

1966 when black rioting struck the city and Mayor Daley called out the National Guard. Pleading for jobs, schools, and housing for the city's blacks, Martin planned to live in a slum tenement in the ghetto to demonstrate for TV the miserable conditions in which inner-city blacks were forced to live.

He demanded that Daley prosecute Chicago's slumlords. Daley merely shrugged and told Martin to "go slow."

Now grown weary from his struggle and under constant threats of death, Martin told one reporter, "Sometimes I doubt whether I'm going to make it through.... I've been hit so many times I'm immune to it. I have been in many demonstrations all across the South, but I have never seen in Alabama and Mississippi mobs as hostile and hate-filled as I have seen in Chicago."

THIRTEEN

PRESIDENT Johnson had done more than any modern president to protect civil rights, and blacks had seen a steady stream of federal laws and Supreme Court decisions passed in their favor. But millions of blacks were embittered when Johnson abandoned his War on Poverty, now spending the funds that had been allocated to help poor blacks on the escalating Vietnam War. Blacks were also growing increasingly impatient and disillusioned with the slow-as-molasses progress toward real equality in their lives.

The intense frustration and dissatisfaction of urban blacks exploded in a series of riots in northern cities that rocked the nation and marked a sharp break with the nonviolent leadership of Martin Luther King. A more militant black mood rapidly became evident. In 1966 even Mississippi blacks staged a Black Power March. Attacked by a white mob armed with hoes and ax handles, they fought back furiously with fists. "I'm committed to nonviolence," declared CORE's Floyd McKissick, "but I say what we need is to get us some black power!" SNCC's chairman Stokely Carmichael became the spokesman of an emerging Black Power movement.

Martin replied:

> It is absolutely necessary for the Negro to gain power, but the term "Black Power" is unfortunate because it tends to give the impression of black nationalism. . . . We must never seek power exclusively for the Negro but the sharing of power with white people. Any other course is exchanging one form of tyranny for another. Black supremacy would be equally as evil as white supremacy.

Black militants like Stokely Carmichael and Bobby Seale considered Martin naive for believing that he could tumble the walls of prejudice by peaceful demonstrations and chants of "We shall overcome." And they considered him unrealistic in urging blacks to love their oppressors. Still, most respected Martin as a dedicated crusader and recognized that no black leader in America commanded greater love and devotion among blacks.

Yet Martin couldn't ignore the voices of opposition in his own organizations. Speaking to a SNCC and CORE rally in Mississippi, he felt hurt when he was booed by some militant blacks.

"I went home that night with an ugly feeling," he recalled later. "Selfishly I thought of my sufferings and sacrifices over the last twelve years. Why would they boo one so close to them? . . . For twelve years, I and others like me had held out radiant promises of progress. . . . Their hopes had soared. They were now booing because they felt we were unable to deliver on our promises."

Martin continued speaking out against the Vietnam War as "a blasphemy against all that America stands for," a war in which blacks were "dying in disproportionate numbers." He led peace demonstrations in New York and San Francisco, upsetting NAACP and Urban League leaders, as well as his own father, all of whom wanted Martin to stick to civil rights issues.

But young antiwar blacks in CORE and SNCC supported him. Bayard Rustin, black leader of the War Resisters League, said the American black was puzzled "to be told he must turn the other cheek in our own South while we must fight for freedom in South Vietnam."

Black rioting and firebombing continued in northern cities, much to the delight of southern segregationists who saw the North "get a taste of their own medicine." The worst riots of the decade occurred during the summer of 1967 in Newark, New Jersey, and Detroit, Michigan. These and other cities were seething with black anger over the severe unemployment among black adults, the lack of opportunities for jobless teenagers, and the brutality of the police.

In Newark a four-day riot in which 21 blacks died was fought by 1,300 police reinforced by 475 state troopers and 4,000 National Guardsmen. To battle the riot in Detroit, Governor George Romney dispatched National Guardsmen in Patton tanks, machine guns blazing. Over 7,200 people were arrested and over 40 were killed.

The rioting and increasing black militant cries of "Black Power" frightened many white Americans, who feared the black crusades had now gone too far. Martin himself was deeply troubled when white northern support for civil rights fell off sharply. Even Congress's support was fading. Having failed to pass the president's 1966 Civil Rights Act, Congress angrily voted it down again following the Newark and Detroit riots.

Now convinced that his crusade had to emphasize not just civil rights but also jobs and economic opportunities for blacks, Martin hit on the idea of a Poor People's March on Washington. The marchers would plead their case with every department of the government, as well as with Congress. On December 4, 1967, Martin announced his plan to bring the march to Washington in April 1968.

"We will place the problems of the poor," Martin wrote, "at the seat of government of the wealthiest nation in the history of mankind."

In February 1968, in one of his most moving and prophetic speeches, Martin let it be known how he wished to be remembered after his death. Not by his Nobel Peace Prize or four hundred other awards, he said. He hoped that people would say:

> Martin Luther King, Jr., tried to give his life serving others. I'd like somebody to say that day that Martin Luther King, Jr., tried to love somebody. . . . I want you to be able to say that day that I did try to feed the hungry. I want you to be able to say that day that I did try in my life to clothe the naked. . . . And I want you to say that I tried to love and save humanity.

That wish would soon have occasion to be remembered vividly.

FOURTEEN

In Memphis, Tennessee, the Sanitation Workers Union, most of whose underpaid members were black, went on strike against a new racist mayor to demand union recognition and benefits equal to those of the all-white police and fire departments. The union begged Martin to come to Memphis to lead a demonstration. He agreed at once, and in March 1968 he was greeted at a union rally with a roar of acclaim.

"The world is changing," he cried to the crowd, "and anyone who thinks he can live alone is sleeping through a revolution. . . . We must learn to live together as brothers or we will perish together as foes. . . . Racial injustice is still the black man's burden and the white man's shame."

Wild enthusiasm greeted his call for a total one-day general strike in Memphis. If the strikers arranged a march for that day, Martin promised he would return to lead it.

Leaving Memphis, he whirled off to Alabama, Mississippi, New York, and New Jersey to recruit volunteers for his Poor People's March. His secretary begged him to rest because Martin's pace was a killing one. "You are all going to kill me anyway," he said with a laugh, "and I'd just as soon die at an early age."

When he returned to Memphis on March 28 to lead the demonstration as he had promised, violence erupted. SCLC aides hustled Martin to a waiting car and sped him to safety. Black Power militants clashed with police, who shot and killed a sixteen-year-old black boy. Fifty people were injured in the melee, and some 120 were arrested. The governor sent 3,800 National Guardsmen into the city, and a dusk-to-dawn curfew was imposed.

Martin was agonized and rendered sleepless by the

violence. He became depressed when Roy Wilkins of the NAACP suggested calling off the Poor People's March in Washington because of Martin's inability to keep the Memphis march peaceful.

Martin immediately announced he would lead a second march in Memphis, and this time, he vowed, it would be kept nonviolent. But when he returned to lead it, he found that the city had won a court injunction against further demonstrations.

Martin did not intend to let that stop him. In a Memphis church he made what proved to be his last speech. He revealed that threats had been made against his life by "some of our sick white brothers."

"I don't know what will happen now," he cried.

We've got some difficult days ahead. But it really doesn't matter with me now, because I've been to the mountaintop, and I don't mind. Like anybody, I would like to live a long life; longevity has its grace. But I'm not concerned about that now. I just want to do God's will. And He's allowed me to go up to the mountain. And I've looked over, and I've seen the promised land. I may not get there with you, but I want you to know tonight that we ,·s a people will get to the promised land. So I'm happy tonight.

There were tears in the eyes of his listeners as he finished.

The following evening, April 4, 1968, as Martin was leaning over the rail of the Lorraine Motel balcony chatting with some followers in the courtyard below, the explosive whine of a rifle bullet was heard. Martin crumpled to the floor, mortally wounded in the head. An hour later he was dead.

His assassin was an escaped white convict, James Earl

Ray, who had fired the shot from a room in a nearby boardinghouse. Escaping in the confusion, he was arrested thirty-four days later in London, but kept silent about his motive. Almost all blacks were certain he had been hired by the fanatical southern segregationists who had been threatening Martin's life.

Ray admitted that he had expected to be allowed to escape because of FBI chief J. Edgar Hoover's hatred for Martin.

Americans were shocked and incredulous at the assassination. Many were still aggrieved over the loss of another beloved leader who had been assassinated five years earlier— President John F. Kennedy. Millions of white Americans who recognized that Martin had been perhaps the nation's best hope of solving the racial problem peacefully, now worried uneasily that blacks would hold all whites responsible for Martin's murder.

Law enforcement authorities throughout the country braced for stormy emotional outbursts in the ghettos. National Guard troops were called up, and the U.S. Army took "precautionary measures" by alerting troops for riot duty. President Johnson summoned civil rights leaders to an emergency session at the White House. He urged them to keep their followers nonviolent, confessing he feared that both blacks and whites might now be convinced that violence was the only solution to race problems.

"That will be nothing less than a catastrophe for our country," Johnson said. "No one could doubt what Martin Luther King would want. That his death should be the cause of more violence would deny everything he worked for."

The president went on TV to proclaim a national day of mourning for Martin Luther King, ordering all American flags flown at half-staff. He also announced that he was calling a special joint session of Congress, at which he planned to urge immediate passage of a new and strong 1968 Civil Rights Act, along with a demand for gun control legislation.

The first reaction of the black community in America to news of the assassination was one of dazed grief. Black dock-workers in New Orleans left the piers for a day of public mourning. Black drivers in Harlem kept their headlights on in daylight to express their anguish and bitterness.

"Dr. Martin Luther King was the last prince of nonviolence," Floyd McKissick declared. "Nonviolence is a dead philosophy, and it was not the black people that killed it."

Black wrath began to explode across the nation. Racial rioting erupted in 125 cities, with buildings going up in flames, wild looting, attacks on police and firemen, and gun battles in the streets. Crowds gathered in the ghettos to listen to furious black speakers denounce white America.

In Washington, D.C., Stokely Carmichael told crowds, "Go home and get your guns! When the white man comes he is coming to kill you. I don't want any black blood in the street!"

"We must move from resistance to aggression," cried Black Panther leader H. Rap Brown, "from revolt to revolution!"

A thick pall of smoke from at least seventy fires set by rioters hung over Washington. Water pressure ran low as firemen fought to keep the whole capital from going up in flames. When the looting and disorders came within two blocks of the White House, the president was forced to declare an emergency.

Army and National Guard troops were called out to protect the capital. Helmeted soldiers with bayonet-fixed rifles guarded the White House itself, and a light machine-gun post defended the steps of the Capitol. Police made over four thousand arrests, and a curfew was imposed for several nights.

Before riots in the nation's ghettos subsided, at least 46 people had been killed, over 2,600 injured, and more than 21,270 arrested. Damage to property was estimated at $67 million. Never before in American history had there been such widespread rioting. The occasion of Martin's assassination had been used to express the desperation of black Americans.

"Martin Luther King was a saint and a martyr," declared one black radical. "But *we* aren't saints, and we don't intend to let the white man make us martyrs!"

On April 23 the *Wall Street Journal* ran an article headlined WHITE RACISM: GHETTO VIOLENCE BRINGS HARDENING OF ATTITUDES TOWARDS NEGRO GROUPS. The article quoted a gun shop clerk as saying, "The word is out that if there's any trouble this summer and you see a black man in your neighborhood, shoot to kill and ask questions later."

Martin was no longer there to cry, "How long, O Lord?"

FIFTEEN

No man contributed more to the great progress of blacks during the fifties and sixties than Martin Luther King. He helped mightily to bring down the structure of Jim Crow in the South. Thanks to his marches and protests, black children were able to attend previously all-white schools. His efforts helped millions of southern blacks to vote and elect blacks to office. New economic opportunities he fostered helped develop a black middle class, which grew from only 5 percent to a third of all black families in just thirty years, an amazing transformation.

Dr. Gunnar Myrdal, the famous Swedish economist who

wrote the classic study of black Americans, *An American Dilemma*, expressed his belief that in the end black extremism would fail, but that Martin Luther King's idealism would prevail.

On January 20, 1986, the U.S. government expressed its appreciation for Martin's crusades by making his birthday a federal holiday—the first such honor bestowed on any black.

Postmortem revelations about Martin revealed that even the great Dr. King had feet of clay. A researcher found that he had plagiarized his doctoral thesis as a young man and that he had not always respected his marriage vows while on the road. But revelations of these all-too-human frailties could not diminish Martin's great accomplishments as a fighter for civil rights.

Twenty years after his murder, *Newsweek* paid him a final tribute:

In twelve years of a turbulent public ministry, Martin Luther King had wrought a revolution. An obscure, in some ways unprepossessing, Alabama preacher with a prophet's sense of destiny and the thrum of Old Testament moral fervor in his throat, he had managed to mold a generation of oppressed black Americans and their white sympathizers into a triumphant army of protest.

Together, King's often bloodied legions breached the exclusionist racial redoubts of the South, integrating classrooms, lunch counters and public-transportation facilities and, ultimately, stirring Congress to enact a voting rights measure that changed the face of Southern political power.

On June 30, 1991, the Lorraine Motel where Martin had been assassinated was turned into the National Civil Rights Museum as a memorial to him. Over a hundred celebrities and civil rights advocates, including Rosa Parks, Coretta Scott King, and Jesse Jackson, attended the ceremony in Nashville, Tennessee.

The body of Martin Luther King, Jr., lies in a crypt in an Atlanta churchyard under the carved words he had quoted in his famous "I Have a Dream" speech in Washington:

FREE AT LAST, FREE AT LAST
THANK GOD ALMIGHTY
I'M FREE AT LAST

(Library of Congress)

Malcolm X

1 9 2 5 – 1 9 6 5

"I Don't Advocate Violence, But..."

ONE

MALCOLM X was stung when *The New York Times* ran a poll of the city's blacks that found Martin Luther King, Jr., chosen by 75 percent as doing the best work for blacks. Only 6 percent voted for Malcolm.

"Do you realize," he told author Alex Haley, who cowrote his autobiography, "that some of history's greatest leaders never were recognized until they were safely in the ground?"

But he was mollified by the *Times*'s observation that while King commanded the allegiance of middle- and upper-class blacks, Malcolm was supported by those in the underclass.

Asked by reporters his view of Martin's nonviolent marches, Malcolm declared that both he and Martin had the same goal of saving America from its racism, but used different approaches. Then he made a prophetic remark to Alex Haley:

> In the racial climate of this country today, it is anybody's guess which of the "extremes" in approach to the black man's problems might *personally* meet a fatal catastrophe first—"nonviolent" Dr. King, or so-called "violent" me. . . . I am only facing the facts when I know that any moment of any day, or any night, could bring me death.

It was Malcolm who was assassinated first.

Like King, Malcolm was an outstanding black leader of the 1950s and 1960s, one who chose a different, militant path to resolve black grievances.

MALCOLM X was born Malcolm Little in Omaha, Nebraska, on May 19, 1925. His father, Earl Little, a one-eyed Baptist minister, was president of the Omaha branch of UNIA and a dedicated organizer for Marcus Garvey. Malcolm often accompanied his father to private UNIA meetings in black homes.

"I remember seeing the big shiny photographs of Marcus Garvey . . . passed from hand to hand," Malcolm recalled. "My father had a big envelope of them that he always took to these meetings." Malcolm was deeply impressed by pictures showing huge black crowds in UNIA parades headed by Garvey, resplendent in a magnificent uniform.

He never forgot his father's dynamic preaching at Baptist church meetings. His father always adjourned with Garvey's rallying cry, "Up, you mighty race, you can accomplish what you want!" Malcolm grew up believing that.

He was aware from earliest childhood of the hazards faced by blacks in a white world. Three of his six uncles were killed by white men, one by lynching. His own home had been attacked by the Ku Klux Klan just weeks before he was born.

Earl Little moved his family to Lansing, Michigan, only to incur the hostility of white racists again for spreading Marcus Garvey's message. When Malcolm was four, members of the Black Legion, who wore black robes instead of the Klan's white, attacked and set fire to the Little house. White police and firemen simply stood aside and watched it burn down. The family had to move twice more to escape further harassment.

There was also trouble within the family. Malcolm's father resented the better education of his second wife, a mulatto from Grenada in the British West Indies. When Earl Little was in a bad mood, he beat her. He also beat his eight children. Because Malcolm's mother whipped him, too, Malcolm accepted violence as part of his childhood.

When he was six, his father was murdered, thrown under a streetcar by white racists.

"It always stayed on my mind that I would die a violent death," he ruminated toward the end of his life. "In fact, it runs in my family. My father and most of his brothers died by violence—my father because of what he believed in. . . . If I take the kind of things in which I believe, then add that to the kind of temperament I have . . . these are the ingredients which make it just about impossible for me to die of old age."

The family lived from hand to mouth as Malcolm's mother took jobs sewing or doing housework for white families. She was often dismissed as soon as it was learned she was the wife of "that trouble-making black minister who stirred up the blacks."

Malcolm grew up on family welfare checks. Often he and his siblings went hungry, sometimes getting through the day on three meals of oatmeal mush. "I was so hungry I didn't know what to do," he recalled. Returning from school, he would often dally at stores to steal fruit. If he was caught, he could expect a whipping from his mother.

In 1936, worn out by the struggle of raising eight children in poverty, his mother began losing her mind. A social worker placed Malcolm with a black family named Gohannas who had been ardent parishioners of his father's.

Then, when his mother was sent to a state mental hospital, Malcolm and his siblings became wards of the state. The family was split up, his brothers and sisters placed with different families. Malcolm turned bitter, blaming the state for destroying his family.

At thirteen he decided to make his way as a boxer. In his first fight he was badly beaten by a white boy, who later knocked him out in a rematch. That convinced Malcolm he didn't belong in a ring. He felt he didn't belong in school, either, misbehaving so badly that he was sent to a detention home in Mason, Michigan.

The Swerlins, a white couple, were in charge of the home, where they often discussed "niggers." Malcolm vividly remembered once hearing Swerlin observe, "I just can't see how those niggers can be so happy and be so poor." Mrs. Swerlin replied, "Niggers are just that way." All through childhood and adolescence Malcolm grew used to the epithet.

He was one of a few black children attending Mason Junior High School. Something of a novelty to the white children, he was treated well and accepted socially.

Mrs. Swerlin got him a job after school earning money washing dishes in a restaurant. Malcolm proved so bright in school that he earned the best grades in the seventh grade and became so popular that he was elected class president.

"I lived a thoroughly integrated life," he said in retrospect. He wryly recalled trying hard, in every way possible, to "be white."

T W O

In 1940, when Malcolm was fifteen, he was invited to visit his half-sister Ella, a daughter of his father's first marriage, who lived in the black Roxbury section of Boston. The small-town boy from the Midwest was fascinated by the sophisticated lives led by Roxbury blacks and found the big city far more exciting than tame, rural Mason.

Returning to school, he remained at the top of his class. His English teacher asked him what career he hoped to pursue. Malcolm confessed his dream of becoming a lawyer.

"That's no realistic goal for a nigger," the teacher scoffed. He suggested that Malcolm pursue carpentry instead. Malcolm was stung, especially since white youngsters with grades inferior to his own were encouraged to pursue professional careers.

Suddenly feeling his "niggerdom" in a white environment, he determined to live in a black society. He managed to have Ella transfer him from Michigan to Massachusetts. Living in Roxbury with her, he was befriended by a pool hall hustler named Shorty, who introduced Malcolm to Roxbury's underworld.

Shorty got Malcolm a job as a shoeshine boy and washroom attendant at the Roseland State Ballroom. But the real money came from black pimps who paid Malcolm to pass their hookers' phone numbers or addresses to white males looking for black prostitutes. Soon Shorty had Malcolm shooting craps, playing the numbers, and drinking and smoking reefers. Malcolm had his kinky hair "conked" into a white man's straight hairstyle and wore a zoot suit, an exaggerated, fancy attire then a popular fad. Still only fifteen, Malcolm loved dancing at the Roseland Ballroom, showing off his slick, "cool cat" style. He felt transformed from a Michigan bumpkin into a sharp Roxburyite.

After working as a shoeshine boy, soda jerk, and busboy, Malcolm lied about his age to get a job as a sandwich vendor on the New York, New Haven & Hartford train running between Boston and Washington. Layovers in Harlem fascinated him so much that he soon moved there. He was thrilled to walk the streets where his hero Marcus Garvey had once staged the great parades that had magnetized Harlem.

Excited by his new life and freedom in New York, Malcolm began drinking and smoking marijuana to excess. Becoming arrogant and insulting toward train passengers, he was fired.

In 1942, now seventeen, Malcolm was hired as a waiter in a Harlem bar, a hangout for underworld figures. They enthralled him with tales of their numbers rackets, pimping, con games, drug peddling, and armed robberies. Malcolm again began making contacts for pimps. But in early 1943, his proposition to one of his customers, a black detective dressed as a serviceman, cost him his job. Giving up legitimate work, Malcolm now fully joined his friends in the criminal underworld.

One friend, a pimp, gave him work peddling marijuana. Malcolm carried a gun for protection. When he became aware that detectives were watching him closely, he stopped selling reefers and turned to armed robbery in nearby cities. To steady his nerves, he began using cocaine and opium.

For the next four years, Malcolm worked as a burglar, a numbers runner, a pimp for a Harlem madam, and a truck driver for bootleggers, often narrowly escaping arrest or death. Finally Malcolm returned to Boston and organized a burglary ring. By that time he was a cocaine addict, desperately needing money for his habit.

One day he made a careless slip that led to the arrest of all involved in his burglary ring. In February 1946, not yet twenty-one, he was sentenced to ten years in Charlestown State Prison.

Malcolm was able to continue his narcotics addiction

behind bars by buying drugs from guards. During his early prison years he was so violent that he was often placed in solitary confinement. Always cursing God and the Bible, he was nicknamed Satan by the other prisoners.

After some time Malcolm fell under the spell of a charismatic black prisoner named Bimbi, who commanded respect from guards and inmates alike with his fluent command of language. Bimbi persuaded Malcolm to use the prison library to improve his knowledge and vocabulary. At Bimbi's urging, Malcolm also took prison correspondence courses so he could complete the education he quit in the eighth grade.

Malcolm became curious about a religion for blacks called the Nation of Islam after receiving a letter from his brother Philbert. Philbert revealed that he and several of his brothers and sisters had converted to it and were now praying for Malcolm's conversion.

Malcolm's curiosity increased after his half-sister Ella arranged his transfer to Norfolk Prison Colony, an experimental institution that emphasized rehabilitation. Here he was visited by his brother Reginald, one of the Muslim converts, who told Malcolm about the new religion. The Muslims followed a black leader, Elijah Muhammad, called "the Messenger of Allah."

Muhammad preached that the black man's rightful place was at the top of society, a place usurped by the "treachery of the blue-eyed devil white man." One day these devils would be overthrown by blacks who were the "Lost-Found Nation of Islam" in North America and the true children of God.

Malcolm's sister Hilda urged him to write to Elijah Muhammad, who himself had been in prison, serving five years for evading the draft. When Malcolm did so, he received a reply enclosing a $5 bill. Muhammad's letter told Malcolm that black men were imprisoned only because of oppression by white men who made them criminals by refusing them jobs.

Impressed, Malcolm now wrote daily letters to Muhammad, steadily improving his writing skills to impress the Black Muslim leader. He immersed himself in books from the prison library, an extensive collection donated by a millionaire, delving especially into black history. Everything he read seemed to document Elijah Muhammad's theory of the white man as devil. Malcolm decided he had been fighting social injustice the wrong way and needed to give up his criminal past. Instead he now planned to challenge the system by helping to build a strong, united Black Muslim brotherhood.

As a devout Muslim, Malcolm worked earnestly to convert other black prisoners. After spending six and a half years in prison, he was finally paroled in 1949.

THREE

FOR most of the next three years he worked as a salesman in the clothing store of his brother Wilfred in the black ghetto of Detroit, while attending the city's Muslim Temple Number One. Malcolm was deeply impressed by the pride the temple's adherents took in being black. In 1952 he rode in a caravan with them to visit Temple Number Two in Chicago to hear Elijah Muhammad speak.

Muhammad's preaching revived Malcolm's childhood memories of his father's proselytizing for Marcus Garvey and UNIA—the message that blacks must not integrate into white society, but build their own black nation. Muhammad said, "The Negro wants to lose his identity because he does not know his identity."

Malcolm was astonished when Muhammad suddenly

called out his name during the service, asking him to stand. Muhammad then told the congregation that Malcolm had written him a daily letter for years, and that the Nation of Islam had led Malcolm to give up drinking, smoking, drugs, and a life of crime.

After the rally Malcolm and the Detroit Muslims were invited to Muhammad's home. Malcolm was encouraged to recruit young blacks for the Detroit temple.

Returning to Detroit, he began a zealous recruiting drive. Renouncing his family name as one bestowed by some "blue-eyed devil" generations earlier, he assumed the new name of Malcolm X. The X stood for his unknown original African family name.

Malcolm disseminated the "good news" of the coming rise of the black man and the fall of the white man. He began his crusade by attacking Christianity as "a religion concocted by the white man . . . designed to make us look down on black and up on white." Christianity, he declared, was nothing but "white supremacy . . . designed to fill [blacks'] hearts with the desire to be white."

He thundered, "Find a black man who has raped a woman, a black man who is a drunk, or a black man in the gutter, and you will find a black man who is a Christian!" The true religion for blacks, Malcolm cried, was only Islam. "It only takes a spark to light the fire," he vowed. "We are that spark!"

In 1953 Malcolm's firebrand recruiting tripled the Detroit temple's membership in just three months. Muhammad praised him warmly and invited Malcolm to dinner whenever he visited Chicago. That year Malcolm was ordained assistant minister of the Detroit temple and sent to Boston and Philadelphia to open new temples.

In 1954 Malcolm was acknowledged as the dynamo of the

Nation of Islam and appointed a full minister of Temple Seven in New York City, then just a little storefront in Harlem. By 1956 the number of temples in the country had grown to fifteen, most organized by Malcolm. Through his recruiting drives, the movement continued to grow into the next decade.

Blacks were galvanized by Malcolm's rallies, laughing at his jibes about the glories of integration: "Imagine, you'll have a chance to go to the toilet with white folks!" They were stirred by his fiery rhetoric. "Revolution is bloody!" he told a Detroit rally. "Revolution is hostile, revolution knows no compromise, revolution overturns and destroys everything that gets in its way!"

Asked if he didn't fear going to jail for such inflammatory statements, Malcolm replied, "The hell that the so-called Negroes have gone through for these many years in North America will make the inside of a jailhouse look like the best suite in the Waldorf-Astoria Hotel!"

Malcolm's growing power and respect was evidenced in Harlem one night in April 1957. Black Muslim Hinton Johnson was watching a street fight when two white policemen ordered him to move away. When he didn't move fast enough, one cop split his scalp with a nightstick and arrested him. Word flashed to Malcolm. He quickly mustered fifty members of Temple Seven.

They gathered ominously outside the police station where the injured Johnson was being held. Malcolm demanded to see him, then insisted he be hospitalized. When an ambulance took Johnson away, Malcolm led a march to Harlem Hospital. Eight hundred angry blacks joined the Muslims in a fifteen-block-long procession. Worried police ordered the crowd to disperse.

But they stayed with Malcolm until he was assured

Johnson was getting proper care and was promised that the brutal cop would be punished. Then, with a wave of his hand, Malcolm dispersed the crowd.

"No man should have that much power," the awed deputy chief inspector of the Twenty-eighth Precinct declared. Harlem was also awed when Malcolm and Johnson later succeeded in suing the police, winning a $70,000 jury award.

Early in 1959 Elijah Muhammad sent Malcolm on a three-week trip to Islamic nations of the Middle East and Africa to gauge how Muhammad would be received there. Malcolm was accompanied by temple member Betty X, a nurse he had married in 1958.

He was granted an audience with President Gamal Abdel Nasser of Egypt and other African leaders. Upon returning, he urged Muhammad to undertake the pilgrimage to Mecca.

"The Holy City of Mecca," Malcolm related later, "had been the first time I had ever stood before the Creator of All and felt like a complete human being. . . . My thinking had been opened wide in Mecca."

Malcolm and Elijah Muhammad received their first major news coverage late in 1959 in a TV documentary called "The Hate That Hate Produced." CBS newsman Mike Wallace described it as "a study of the rise of black racism . . . of a call for black supremacy . . . among a small but growing segment of the American Negro population."

"[The Black Muslims] claim a membership of at least a quarter of a million Negroes," Wallace told the CBS audience. "Their doctrine is being taught in fifty cities across the nation. Let no one underestimate the Muslims. They have their own parochial schools, like this one in Chicago, where Muslim children are taught to hate the white men. . . . They have their own stores, supermarkets, barbershops, restaurants . . . even a Muslim department store."

As the documentary flashed a picture of Malcolm, Wallace said, "Here you see their minister, Malcolm X, proudly displaying five of the biggest Negro papers in America . . . papers published in Los Angeles, New York, Pittsburgh, Detroit, and Newark. Negro politicians, regardless of their private belief, listen when the leaders of the Black Supremacist movement speak."

Wallace added that at a future rally Muhammad planned to call for "the destruction of the white man." Interviewing Malcolm with the permission of Elijah Muhammad, Wallace asked his opinion of the NAACP.

"Most organizations that represent the so-called Negro," Malcolm replied, "usually we find when we study them that though they are supposed to be for us, the leadership or the brain power or the political power or whatever power that runs it usually is the white man."

Newspapers reported the broadcast, and weekly magazines ran stories calling the Black Muslims "hate-teaching racists" and "black fascists" who urged violence against whites.

When leaders of other black organizations rushed to denounce the Muslims and disclaim their views, Malcolm scornfully dismissed them as "Uncle Toms."

Asked by reporters if it was true that he and the Muslims hated whites, Malcolm replied, "For the white man to ask the black man if he hates him is just like the rapist asking the *raped*, or the wolf asking the *sheep*, 'Do you hate me?' The white man is in no moral *position* to accuse anyone else of hate!"

In a *Playboy* interview, Malcolm declared that if the present generation of whites studied the truth about their own race history, it would make them antiwhite themselves.

FOUR

WITH the intensive national coverage given to the Black Muslims, Malcolm was able to influence more black listeners to join the Nation of Islam. In rallies held four or five times a year in New York, Chicago, and Washington, big halls now overflowed with audiences of ten thousand and more. At first no white persons were admitted to the rallies, which Malcolm considered poetic justice—paying whites back for their years of segregation.

The rallies opened with a Black Muslim song, "White Man's Heaven Is Black Man's Hell." Then Malcolm would make a highly emotional speech to introduce the man who had rescued him from an evil life when he had been a convict and who had treated him personally like a son.

Elijah Muhammad would urge blacks to join the Muslims and grow their own food, build factories to manufacture their own goods, set up their own stores, conduct their own commerce, and eventually develop an independent black nation.

Police and the FBI now paid close attention to this mass movement. They constantly interrogated Malcolm and Muhammad and tapped their phones, seeking incriminating evidence that would lead to arrests. The FBI kept files on Malcolm's speeches, recording such "subversive" remarks as his admonition to blacks, "You hear us talking about the white man and you want to go away and tell him we have been subversive. Here is a man who raped your mother and hung your father on his tree; is *he* subversive?" The FBI also quoted Malcolm as saying, "The white man has so thoroughly brainwashed the Negro that he wants to be like everyone but himself."

By 1961 the Nation of Islam had expanded the number of Muslim-owned small businesses in many cities that employed and traded only with blacks. In Detroit black children could attend Muslim elementary and junior high schools; in Chicago they could go from kindergarten through high school. From the earliest grades they were taught both black history and Arabic.

The Nation of Islam also developed an effective program for curing drug addicts who became members. Malcolm blamed alcoholism and drug addiction on the self-hatred that whites had instilled in blacks. He helped induce them to stop buying "Whitey's dope" and doing "Whitey's bidding" by killing themselves with addiction.

Malcolm's success as an organizer led Muhammad in 1962 to award him a car and house, support for his family, and freedom to travel wherever he wished. Muhammad also promoted him to national minister of the Temple of Islam.

As national minister Malcolm announced an international goal: "Blue-eyed white devils have gained control of the world, subjugating the black race. Thus blacks need to unify, revolt and build a proud separate society." He declared in May, "What is looked upon as an American dream for white people has long been an American nightmare for black people."

When Muhammad moved to Arizona for his health, he appointed Malcolm to represent him more and more on radio and TV. Speaking to black and white students in over fifty colleges and universities around the country, Malcolm made his message clear.

At a Michigan State University lecture on January 23,

1963, he told his audience that the Muslims were now the fastest-growing religious group among blacks anywhere in the Western hemisphere. "I'm letting you know," he said, "how a black man thinks, how a black man feels, and how dissatisfied black men should have been four hundred years ago."

He scoffed at "Uncle Toms" ashamed of being black for seeking integration with whites, and eulogized blacks proud of their African heritage and ancient culture who wanted control of a separate community all their own. "The unity of Africans abroad and the unity of Africans here in this country," he declared, "can bring about any kind of achievement or accomplishment that black people want today."

At the University of California in October 1962 he attacked the liberals' "great fuss over the South only to blind us to what is happening here in the North. . . . America now faces a race war. The entire country is on the verge of erupting into racial violence and bloodshed simply because twenty million ex-slaves here in America are demanding freedom, justice, and equality from their former slavemasters."

The solution, Malcolm said, was "some land that we can call our own. Then we can create our own jobs. Control our own economy. Solve our own problems. . . . The Honorable Elijah Muhammad teaches us that on our own land we can set up farms, factories, businesses. We can establish our own government and become an independent nation."

Speaking at Boston University, he told students that he was proud to be known as "the angriest Negro in America."

That anger burst forth after a clash between Black Muslims and police in Los Angeles that year left one black dead and a dozen wounded. Only the restraint of other temple leaders stopped a furious Malcolm from leading Muslims in an armed attack on the police.

FIVE

N o w much in the limelight, Malcolm was accused of dividing the black community, pitting those working for the betterment of blacks within white society against those seeking a separate black state.

Malcolm also leveled criticism at Martin Luther King. As early as 1958, he called Martin "a professional Negro. . . . His profession is being a Negro for the white man." Later, considering the violence blacks endured peacefully in the South during King's demonstrations, Malcolm argued, "No man can speak for Negroes who tells Negroes love your enemy. . . . There's no Negro in his right mind today who's going to tell Negroes to turn the other cheek."

He angered many blacks by deriding Martin as a "chump," ridiculing the notion that the American government would ever agree to major social reforms without the threat of a black uprising. He held up as evidence the slow actions of President Kennedy, whom four out of five blacks had voted for in the 1960 election. Malcolm observed acidly in 1963, "Those who are familiar with Kennedy's promises to the Negro know what he said he could do with the stroke of his pen. And he was in office for two years before he found where his fountain pen was."

Malcolm also criticized the Freedom Riders, claiming that by going south they were ignoring black oppression in northern ghettos. "Everything south of the Canadian border," he scoffed, is 'South.' "

By this time Malcolm was recognized as the militant champion of ghetto blacks. As he defiantly told his college audiences, "Gentlemen, I finished the eighth grade in Mason, Michigan. My high school was the black ghetto in Roxbury,

Massachusetts. My college was in the streets of Harlem, and my master's was taken in prison."

When Martin Luther King, Jr., led his march on Washington on August 8, 1963, Malcolm attended to "observe that circus." He scoffed, "How was a one-day 'integrated' picnic going to counter-influence these representatives of prejudice rooted deep in the psyche of the American white man for four hundred years?"

After Freedom Riders met with violence in the South, Malcolm urged greater black militancy. "In the areas of the country where the government had proved itself unable, or unwilling, to defend the Negroes when they are brutally and unjustly attacked," he said, "then the Negroes themselves should take whatever steps are necessary to defend themselves."

Meanwhile, he continued his organizing efforts, which had raised membership in the Nation of Islam from four hundred to forty thousand.

Malcolm was well aware that, as an aggressive black militant, he was putting his life at risk. In 1963 an Associated Press dispatch reported that a chapter of the Louisiana Citizens Council had put up a $10,000 reward for his death.

Malcolm's devout faith in Muhammad was suddenly shaken by reading in a United Press International dispatch that the sixty-seven-year-old black leader was the target of paternity suits by two of his former secretaries, both in their twenties. They charged that he had fathered their four children over the course of six-year affairs.

Malcolm was stunned by the allegations against his idol. From the time he first became a Black Muslim, Malcolm had believed in Muhammad not only as a human leader, but as a divine prophet, incapable of human weakness. Malcolm himself had been a totally faithful family man, devoted to his wife and four daughters, always obeying the strict morality that Muhammad preached.

Unwilling to believe the secretaries' accusations, Malcolm felt that they had to be part of some kind of police, FBI, or white racist frame-up to discredit the Nation of Islam. He rushed to Washington to talk to Muhammad's son Wallace and offer help in scotching the story. To his amazement Wallace told him that Muhammad wanted no such effort made. It became painfully clear to Malcolm that the charges were true.

Malcolm tried to make the best of the situation in his speeches by stressing that a man's lifetime accomplishments ought to outweigh any human weakness. He even found biblical parallels to validate his point—Moses's leading the Hebrews was more significant than his adultery with Ethiopian women; Noah's building the ark was more memorable than his alcoholism; David's slaying of Goliath meant more than his adultery with Bathsheba.

When Malcolm flew to Phoenix to see Muhammad in April 1963, he suggested these parallels as a moral defense. His emotions were mixed when Muhammad fully agreed with them and actually compared himself to Moses, Noah, and David.

Another stunning event occurred on November 22, when Lee Harvey Oswald assassinated President John F. Kennedy. Questioned for comment by reporters, Malcolm called the assassination retribution for the climate of white violence in America—"the chickens coming home to roost." This callous statement made headlines all over the country.

Malcolm was summoned to Phoenix by Muhammad, who reproached him for his insensitive and ill-timed remark,

Malcolm X and Congressman Adam Clayton Powell, Jr., of Harlem, who was elected to Congress for eleven consecutive terms. *(UPI/Bettmann)*

which reflected poorly on the Black Muslims. He was ordered to remain silent for three months, a punishment that would be announced to the press and to members of the Nation of Islam.

But Malcolm began to suspect that Muhammad was simply using the incident as an excuse to get rid of him for fear that Malcolm was overshadowing him and might use the issue of Muhammad's immorality to split the Nation of Islam.

Some Black Muslims felt Malcolm's punishment was meant to show Muhammad's displeasure with him for abandoning his religious message to emphasize the civil rights struggle and black nationalism.

Malcolm subsequently heard that one of his own assistants had been telling some of his congregation, "If you know what the minister [Malcolm] did, you'd go out and kill him yourself." Malcolm was prison-wise enough to understand that such incitement could have emanated from only one source—the highest.

Finding himself threatened by his own movement, Malcolm watched his back carefully.

S I X

MALCOLM'S association with the world-famous boxer Cassius Clay brought him into the spotlight again. Malcolm had gladly accepted an invitation from Clay to vacation with his family at Clay's training camp in Miami, where the boxer was preparing for his heavyweight championship fight with Sonny Liston.

When Clay won the title fight, he announced publicly that he had become a Muslim with the adopted name of Muhammad Ali. This in itself raised eyebrows among his fans, but a public uproar erupted when Ali used his new religion as his reason for refusing to be drafted to fight in Vietnam. As the source of Ali's conversion, Malcolm became even more controversial.

Malcolm learned of a plot to kill him from the very hit man assigned to carry it out. The man, a Black Muslim who respected Malcolm, had been ordered to wire explosives to Malcolm's car. Who had ordered the hit was not disclosed, but Malcolm knew now for certain that his assassination was only a matter of time, unless he took some drastic action. He decided the time had come for an open break with Elijah Muhammad.

Taking some fifty followers with him, in March 1964 he called a meeting in Harlem to announce his defection. He established a new mosque in New York called the Muslim Mosque, Inc., "for blacks regardless of their religious or political beliefs."

His program called for eliminating the political oppression, economic exploitation, and social degradation suffered by millions of black Americans. Warning that "a bloodbath is on its way in America," he urged blacks to seize control of their communities and form armed resistance groups for protection.

"Whites can help us," he told the press conference, "but they can't join us. There can be no black-white unity until there is first some black unity. There can be no workers' solidarity until there is first some racial solidarity. We cannot think of uniting with others, until we have first united among ourselves."

Muhammad was reportedly embittered by Malcolm's "treachery." Malcolm prudently now kept a bodyguard around him at all times.

His new rival organization attracted many blacks who had

been unwilling to join the Nation of Islam because of its demand that they renounce premarital sex, smoking, drinking, gambling, and other violations of the Islamic code. Thousands of ghetto blacks now flocked to Malcolm, enthralled by his eloquent articulation of their gut feelings.

"My hobby," Malcolm said with a smile, "is stirring up Negroes."

In the spring of 1964 he made a second speaking tour to Africa and the Middle East to promote black consciousness. He received approval to make a *Hajj* (pilgrimage) to Mecca, the religious obligation of Muslims to make, if possible, at least once in a lifetime.

Flying to Mecca, he was invited into the plane's cockpit as an honored guest, and was thrilled to see two Egyptians with darker skins than his own at the controls. He had never before seen a black man flying a jet.

En route he was overwhelmed by the great hospitality, kindness, and brotherly feeling shown to him by Muslims with lighter skin. Malcolm now felt compelled to rethink his hostility toward all whites. He began to adjust his concept of "white" as meaning those who had racist attitudes toward people of color, rather than just those with white skins. Arab friends taught him that the descendants of the prophet Muhammad were both black and white, and that Muslims made no distinction between the two, except when they had been corrupted by Western influence.

Prince Faisal of Saudi Arabia sent a special car to take Malcolm to Mecca for the *Hajj*. Malcolm participated in the religious ceremonies along with thousands of praying pilgrims. Afterward he was asked, as a famous Muslim from America, what had impressed him most about the *Hajj*.

"The *brotherhood!*" he exclaimed. "The people of all

races, colors, from all over the world coming together as *one!*"
He found himself deeply stirred by the color-blindness of the
Muslim world. For the first time in his life it had made him
feel like "a complete human being."

"America needs to understand Islam," he wrote home,
"because this is the one religion that erases from its society
the race problem. . . . What I have seen, and experienced, has
forced me to *re-arrange* much of my thought-patterns previously held, and to toss aside some of my previous
conclusions."

During his time of reflection in Mecca, he also realized
that he had made a serious mistake in regarding Elijah Muhammad as a divine leader who could do no wrong. "There
on a Holy World hilltop," he wrote later, "I realized how very
dangerous it is for people to hold any human being in such
esteem."

Wherever Malcolm spoke in the Middle East and Africa,
he was asked about racial prejudice in America. He would
reply that it was worse than his listeners could possibly
imagine.

"I'm not anti-American," he declared in one speech, "and
I didn't come here to *condemn* America—I want to make that
very clear! I came here to tell the truth—and if the *truth*
condemns America, then she stands condemned!"

On another occasion he declared, "I'm black first. My
sympathies are black, my allegiance is black, my whole objectives are black. . . . I am not interested in being American,
because America has never been interested in me."

Malcolm met ambassadors and ministers from lands with
nonwhite populations who expressed concern at the plight of
American blacks. Malcolm reflected how little blacks in the
United States, who saw themselves only as a powerless

minority, realized the great support they had from the world's huge nonwhite majority.

He decided that American blacks had to be made to think globally and seek alliances with other nonwhite nations. "On the world stage," he wrote, "the white man is just a microscopic minority."

Malcolm received a tremendous reception in Ghana, where he was hailed as a militant leader fighting the brutalization of American blacks. Questioned about his break with Elijah Muhammad, Malcolm tried to avoid criticizing him or the Nation of Islam, simply explaining their differences as political.

When he was reprimanded for using the term "Negro," Malcolm began referring to American blacks instead as "Afro-Americans," signifying their cultural link to Africa.

In conversations with Ghana President Kwame Nkrumah, he agreed that a movement of "Pan-Africanism" was basic to dealing with problems of all with African heritage.

Thrilled with his journeys, Malcolm returned home an "orthodox" Muslim. But upon his arrival on May 21, 1964, he found that the ghettos had begun to explode over accumulated grievances. And the press was blaming him for the violence.

SEVEN

As the symbol of black uprising, Malcolm was besieged by reporters. He told them that his Muslim Mosque was now religiously affiliated with 750 million Muslims of the Islamic world and that black Africans regarded America's twenty-two million blacks as their "long-lost brothers."

He was asked about his publicized letter from Mecca stating that he now accepted white men as brothers. "In the past,

During his trip to Cairo in June 1964, Malcolm X meets with Sheik Abdel Rahman Tag, right, future rector of the Muslim university Al Azhar. Malcolm X's meetings with African religious leaders and heads of state changed his views on black-white relations. *(UPI/Bettmann)*

yes, I have made sweeping indictments of *all* white people,"
he admitted. "I never will be guilty of that again—as I know
now that some white people *are* truly sincere, that some truly
are capable of being brotherly toward a black man. . . . To
judge a man because he's white gives him no out. He can't
stop being white. That's like judging us because we're black."

Malcolm emphasized that his fight was not against all
whites, but only against white racists. "We will work with
anyone, with any group, no matter what their color is, as long
as they are genuinely interested in taking the types of steps
necessary to bring an end to the injustices that black people
in this country are afflicted by."

These statements, reported in the press and on TV news,
created something of a sensation. Once, while Malcolm
stopped his car for a traffic light, another car drove alongside
and the white driver put out his hand. "Do you mind shaking
hands with a white man?" the driver said with a grin.

Malcolm laughed. "I don't mind shaking hands with
human beings. Are you one?"

At Harlem meetings of the Muslim Mosque, Malcolm
now invited everyone to attend, regardless of religion or color.

Meanwhile, Harlem's ghetto began erupting with gunfire
and flames. As arsonists torched stores, rioters attacked police
with bottles and other missiles, yelling, "Whitey, we gonna
get you!" Police charged and bloodied them with nightsticks.
The Harlem riot touched off others in Brooklyn, Rochester,
Chicago, Philadelphia, and three New Jersey cities.

Many people who had listened to Malcolm speak now
realized that his rhetoric was based on the harsh truth of bitter
black experience. However, the press continued to blame him
for inciting the violence by telling blacks to use arms to defend
themselves. The FBI alerted its agencies and local police in

many cities to watch for blacks buying firearms and forming rifle clubs.

Malcolm flared:

> If it must take violence to get the black man his human rights in this country, I'm for violence exactly as you know the Irish, the Poles, or Jews would be if they were flagrantly discriminated against . . . no matter what the consequences, no matter who was hurt by the violence. . . . Why was it that when Negroes did start revolting across America, virtually all of white America was caught up in surprise and even shock? . . . We're non-violent with people who are non-violent with us. But we are *not* non-violent with anyone who is violent with us.

Malcolm went abroad again in June 1964 to attend the second meeting of the Organization of African Unity in Cairo. He stayed four months, meeting with such heads of state as Nasser of Egypt, Nyerere of Tanzania, Azikiwe of Nigeria, Nkrumah of Ghana, Touré of Guinea, Kenyatta of Kenya, and Obote of Uganda. He sought their support in creating closer bonds with Afro-Americans.

A new concept in his thinking came from a discussion with a white ambassador in Africa who told Malcolm he never noticed color as long as he was in Africa, but instantly became conscious of it as soon as he returned to America. Malcolm came to the conclusion that racism was not a prejudice natural to white men, but was only the result of a national culture and atmosphere that fostered racism.

"Indeed," he wrote, "how *can* white society atone for enslaving, for raping, for unmanning, for otherwise brutalizing *millions* of human beings for centuries? . . . A desegregated cup of coffee, a theatre, public toilets—the whole range of hypocritical 'integration'—these are not atonement."

He returned from Africa sporting a new reddish mustache and goatee, as though to indicate a changed persona.

In June 1964 he created an Organization of Afro-American Unity (OAAU). Still accused of being antiwhite because of his former "blue-eyed white devil" speeches, Malcolm tried to explain that he now believed in a brotherhood of all races, including whites. However, he declared, before this was possible, Marcus Garvey's teachings of black nationalism first had to be realized. Only when black people achieved racial dignity, pride, confidence, incentive, and unity, he said, could they then welcome unity with white brothers on an equal basis.

For that reason, Malcolm said, white liberals were not permitted to join the OAAU. He urged them instead to prove their sincere concern for civil rights "out on the battle lines of where America's racism really is—and that's in their own home communities."

Malcolm was embittered when Elijah Muhammad instituted a court action to remove him and his family from the Elmhurst, New York, home provided for them by the Nation of Islam.

No longer worshipful of his former idol, Malcolm now began making speeches attacking Muhammad for "religious fakery" and "immorality." He gave incriminating testimony to the attorney general of Illinois, who was investigating the Nation of Islam, and also to the attorney for the two former secretaries who accused Muhammad of fathering their children.

Malcolm began receiving telephoned death threats.

A clash between Muhammad's followers and some of

Malcolm's OAAU members led to the arrest of six of the latter for carrying concealed weapons. Men with knives also attacked a car believed to be transporting Malcolm. And wherever he went, menacing members of the Nation of Islam turned up. Malcolm kept an automatic carbine at home and showed his wife how to use it.

"Black men are watching every move I make," he declared, "awaiting their chance to kill me.... Anyone who chooses not to believe what I am saying doesn't know the Muslims in the Nation of Islam."

E I G H T

WHEN Martin Luther King was jailed in Selma, Alabama, on February 1, 1965, two members of SNCC invited Malcolm there, to the consternation of Martin's SCLC. Malcolm sent a wire ahead to George Lincoln Rockwell, head of the American Nazi party, warning him that if anything happened to blacks in Alabama, he could expect "maximum retaliation" from the OAAU. When Rockwell and his racists failed to intervene in Selma, Malcolm took credit for scaring them off.

Local police looked on grimly as reporters gathered around Malcolm in Selma. He told the newsmen bluntly, "When you're looking at the cops in Alabama, you're looking at the Klan." He reminded them that President Johnson had promised, if elected, to "pull the sheets off the Ku Klux Klan." Malcolm demanded an immediate government investigation of the Klan.

If the government refused, he declared, "then we would be within our rights to come to Alabama and organize the black people of Alabama and pull the sheets off the Klan ourselves!"

Speaking at the mass rally in support of Martin and the

other civil rights demonstrators in prison, Malcolm sought to make Martin's peaceful disobedience look desirable in contrast to his own tougher tactics.

"I don't advocate violence," he said, "but if a man steps on my toes, I'll step on his. . . . Whites better be glad Martin Luther King is rallying the people, because other forces are waiting to take over if he fails!"

Returning to New York, Malcolm flew to France to speak to a Congress of African Students. The French refused to let him speak, however, barring his entry into their country as an "undesirable person."

After a short detour to London, Malcolm returned home on February 13, 1965. In the middle of that night flaming gas bombs crashed through his front window, setting the house on fire. His home half destroyed, Malcolm placed his frightened wife and four small daughters with friends. He was infuriated when Muhammad told reporters Malcolm had firebombed the house himself to get publicity.

"I've reached the end of my rope!" he cried hoarsely to a Harlem audience of five hundred blacks. "I wouldn't care for myself if they would not harm my family! My house was bombed by the Muslims!" He accused Muhammad of also having ordered his officials to kill or maim any Nation of Islam members who had left to follow Malcolm. Branding the Nation of Islam a "criminal organization that used the same tactics as the Klan," he warned grimly, "There are hunters; there are also those who hunt the hunters!"

He told his listeners that when Marcus Garvey had tried to unite American blacks with their African counterparts, "the government framed him and put him in jail. . . . [They] fear that you and I, once we get united, will also unite with our [African] brothers and sisters. . . . This has been the purpose of the OAAU and also the Muslim Mosque—to give us direct links . . . and cooperation with our brothers and sisters all over the earth."

Malcolm told a close friend that he intended to announce the names of the Black Muslim hit men at the next OAAU meeting.

In an interview with Gordon Parks, he told the black *Life* photographer and author, "I did many things as a Muslim that I'm sorry for now. I was a zombie then—like all Muslims— I was hypnotized, pointed in a certain direction and told to march. Well, I guess a man's entitled to make a fool of himself if he's ready to pay the cost. It cost me twelve years!"

On February 16, in a speech at the Corn Hill Methodist Church in New York, he accused France of having barred him from speaking out of fear that blacks in the French West Indies might be inflamed into rebelling by his rhetoric. All the Western powers including the United States, Malcolm charged, were alarmed by the growing unity and militancy of blacks all over the world.

"[We must] make the world see that our problem was no longer a Negro problem or an American problem but a human problem—a problem for humanity," he cried. Blacks needed "people who are in such positions that they can help us get some kind of adjustment for this situation before it gets so explosive that no one can handle it."

On February 21 he drove to the Audubon Ballroom in Harlem to give another speech. Irritated by the refusal of the press to take his claims of death threats seriously, he barred all reporters from the meeting. Before it opened, he told an assistant that he now intended to apologize for having accused the Black Muslims of firebombing his home. More powerful forces were at work, he hinted, implying Hoover's FBI.

As he prepared to speak, a man at the rear of the auditorium yelled at a man beside him, "Take your hands out of my pocket!"

A commotion erupted. Malcolm shouted, "Hold it! Hold it! Don't get excited. Let's cool it, brothers—"

Those were his last words. A smoke bomb went off. As Malcolm's guards rushed to the rear of the auditorium, three men in the front row suddenly rose and aimed guns at Malcolm.

Two of the men, one with a sawed-off shotgun, the other with two revolvers, rushed toward the stage firing their weapons.

Malcolm fell over the chairs behind him as sixteen bullets and shotgun pellets ripped into his body. His wife flew to him from the audience crying, "My husband! They're killing my husband!"

Malcolm died that afternoon in a hospital.

NINE

WHEN the news flashed around Harlem that Malcolm had been assassinated, sorrowing and furious crowds gathered in the streets. Hundreds of extra policemen were posted to prevent a riot.

"Malcolm died according to his preaching," said Elijah Muhammad coldly. "He seems to have taken weapons as his god. Therefore, we couldn't tolerate a man like that. He preached war. We preach peace." That night Muhammad's Black Mosque Number Seven in Harlem was firebombed and destroyed.

Several black Harlem churches refused to conduct the funeral services for Malcolm. When one minister finally agreed, he and his wife received anonymous bomb threats.

Black notables expressed the community's reaction to Malcolm's assassination. Novelist James Baldwin called it "a major setback for the Negro movement." CORE's James Farmer said, "Malcolm's murder was calculated to produce more violence and murder and vengeance killings." The NAACP's Roy Wilkins declared, "Master spell-binder that he was, Malcolm X in death cast a spell more far-flung and more disturbing than any he cast in life."

The African press mourned Malcolm's loss. A Nigerian paper called him "a dedicated and consistent disciple of the movement for the emancipation of his brethren. . . . He will have a place in the palace of martyrs." A Ghana paper ranked him with John Brown and Patrice Lumumba (allegedly murdered by the CIA in the Congo), "who were martyred in freedom's cause."

Three Black Muslims, one of whom was arrested at the murder scene, were indicted for Malcolm's murder on March 10. Elijah Muhammad denied that the Nation of Islam was responsible, saying "His foolish teaching brought him to his own end. . . . He had no right to reject me!"

Twenty thousand Harlemites viewed Malcolm's body as it lay in a chapel. Telegrams and cables of condolence came from Martin Luther King, Jr., every major civil rights organization, and all the African and Middle East kings, presidents, and ministers Malcolm had come to know. Ghana's President Nkrumah's cable read: "The death of Malcolm X shall not have been in vain."

In a funeral elegy actor Ossie Davis cried, "Malcolm was our manhood, our living, black manhood! This was his meaning to his people. And in honoring him, we honor the best in ourselves. . . . [He] didn't hesitate to die, because he loved us so."

Malcolm X's vision lived on as a symbol of the black separatist movement. Others took up his crusade for black self-respect, self-reliance, and economic improvement. They also pursued his later goals—the "human rights" of full employment, with no one, especially children, allowed to go hungry.

In December 1967 a Malcolm X Society was formed, issuing a "declaration of independence" that called for a separate black nation made up of five southern states. Robert Williams, a black ex-Marine refugee in Cuba who headed the Revolutionary Action Movement, was named president-in-exile, with black radical H. Rap Brown as minister of defense.

"We can hold the cities *gloriously*—for about one week," scoffed Richard Henry, cofounder of the Malcolm X Society. "Then we run out of food." He advocated instead a solution more in keeping with Malcolm's views—electing enough black mayors and sheriffs to win control of sufficient law enforcement units to hold off white troops until sympathetic nations came to their aid.

After Malcolm's death, black leaders Bobby Seale and Huey Newton formed the militant Black Panthers. They strove to win black control of America's ghettos, serve poor black families, and defend the ghettos with arms against police brutality and FBI harassment.

"We felt ourselves," Bobby Seale told me, "to be the heirs to Malcolm X."

Thirty years after Malcolm's murder, well after the FBI had destroyed the Black Panthers, Bobby Seale told me, "We have documentation that the FBI's COINTEL program indirectly had something to do with it. They bragged that they helped get Malcolm X."

Malcolm's eldest daughter, Attillah Shabazz, complained

ABOVE, two policemen carry a stretcher bearing Malcolm X after he was downed by an assassin's bullet at Harlem's Audubon Ballroom. *(UPI/Bettmann)* BELOW, members of the Black Panther party demonstrate outside the court where Huey Newton is being tried. *(UPI/Bettmann)*

that her father's posthumous disciples misunderstood his message. Those young blacks, she told the *Los Angeles Times*, were "inspired by pieces of him instead of the entire man. . . . They think 'by any means necessary' means with a gun, as opposed to with a book or getting an 'A' in school."

Malcolm also lived on in rap songs, films, and books preaching his message of black self-respect, self-reliance, and economic empowerment. On TV he was commemorated in music videos produced by rap artists, some of whom dedicated albums to him.

Black film producer Spike Lee's movie *Do the Right Thing* contrasted Martin Luther King's doctrine of nonviolence with Malcolm's doctrine "by any means necessary," posing a debate still being waged in America's black community. Lee also produced a film about Malcolm X, funded in part by famous figures in the black community.

Black America is also still debating whether Malcolm X was right in demanding black separation from white society, or Martin Luther King in demanding full integration.

Like Martin, Malcolm had also had a dream.

"Sometimes," Malcolm mused in the year he died, "I have dared to dream to myself that one day, history may even say that my voice—which disturbed the white man's smugness, and his arrogance, and his complacency—that my voice helped to save America from a grave, possibly even a fatal catastrophe."

The assassinations of Malcolm, Martin, and Medgar Evers, all battlers in the struggle against racism, were reminders of the thousands of lesser-known blacks beaten, mutilated, and murdered in the same struggle.

One can wonder whether, if Malcolm X had lived on into the 1990s, his ability to inspire and win the confidence of young frustrated ghetto blacks might have been able to swing many away from the crack epidemic and street crime into productive lives for themselves.

The young ghetto blacks could believe and follow a man who had been there himself as an underworld pimp, dope addict, con man, armed robber, and convict, and who had then transformed himself into a world-famous, respected black leader, entirely on his own initiative.

What he could do, they could do, too.

The
Black Struggle
Today and
Tomorrow

ONE

''T H E civil rights movement today," John E. Jacob, President of the National Urban League, told me in May 1991, "is fighting a two-front war: to defend past civil rights against reactionary attempts to reverse them, and to help African Americans achieve parity in such crucial areas as employment and education."

He added, "It should be remembered that the original goals of the movement encompassed civil rights and economic equity; the March on Washington was for 'jobs and freedom,' and not solely for narrowly defined civil rights."

James Johnson, director of the Center for the Study of Urban Poverty at UCLA, charged that the two terms of the Reagan administration had declared "open season" on black Americans.

"The eighties gave people license to act upon their racial prejudices," he said. According to government statistics compiled at the beginning of the 1990s, almost half of this country's black children lived below the poverty line. Over twice as many black babies died as white babies. Two out of five black children became school dropouts. Almost one in four black men aged twenty to twenty-nine were either in prison, on parole, or on probation. Because blacks often cannot afford private lawyers, they are six times as likely to go to jail for a criminal charge as whites. And blacks generally receive longer sentences.

Many blacks today no longer look upon a prison record as a badge of shame, but as part of the black experience.

"When you hear that twenty-five of your colleagues are in the criminal justice system—your buddies and friends—it's no longer a big deal," observes black Congressman John

Conyers of Michigan. "In some places it's a badge of merit."

Black children in the inner city become aware from their earliest years of the stigma that white Americans who control the country attach to color. Feeling excluded from American society, they grow up angry. Like Malcolm X, many turn to antisocial acts out of resentment and despair, which only serves to heighten white prejudice.

Young blacks who try to improve their prospects by studying hard, speaking well, and making school honor rolls are often scoffed at by inner-city peers for trying to "act white."

But the black condition in America is a two-sided coin. Even as half the blacks sink deeper into poverty and despair, the other half are realizing the American dream. Millions of black Americans, by dint of hard work, courageous persistence in the face of racism, and the aid of affirmative action laws have steadily developed into a black middle class. From 1960 to 1992 it had grown from just 5 percent to almost half of America's thirty million blacks.

Most of these are beneficiaries of the integrationist dreams of Frederick Douglass and Martin Luther King, Jr. But many still consider that equality with whites has still not been achieved. In a 1991 USA Today poll readers were asked whether they thought blacks were better off in 1991 than during the 1970s, the decade after the height of the civil rights movement. On every issue—employment, social and economic status, education, housing—most whites considered that blacks had made considerable progress, while only half as many blacks agreed.

Advancing to the middle class does not automatically ensure blacks of respectful treatment. Many with good incomes complain of white suspicion and harassment while shopping or banking, simply because of their color.

"What it does to our collective psyche," declared Dr. Alvin Poussaint of Harvard University, "is that it makes sure you never forget that you are black and not welcomed. It is a constant reminder that you live in a society with stereotypes of blacks that you are not free from."

I asked former Executive Director Benjamin L. Hooks what the NAACP saw as the most pressing needs of civil rights legislation tomorrow. "The civil rights movement," he replied, "must confront the indifference or hostility of some whites and the feelings of some blacks that battles have been won. We continue to believe the need for vigilance remains. Equity in our society continues to be a need and priority."

States, cities, and communities have a responsibility to enforce civil rights, not merely to reduce ghetto crime and violence, but as a matter of simple American justice. At the same time the major responsibility must fall on the federal government, which has the superior power and finances necessary to give blacks the same opportunities as whites.

For blacks, the struggle continues as to which way to pursue their goals—through the legacy of integration left them by Frederick Douglass and Martin Luther King, Jr., or the legacy of separatism left them by Marcus Garvey and Malcolm X. Most of those who have prospered through integration choose that way, although an influential coterie of black filmmakers and music celebrities want a separate black society. Most blacks trapped in ghetto poverty and discrimination also opt for separatism, but those inspired with hope by black leaders like Jesse Jackson and successful black businesspeople, athletes, and civic leaders put their faith in the way of Douglass and King.

T W O

T H E president is the most important figure in the nation in setting the agenda on race. George Bush had a mixed record in this respect. While he was only the third president to veto major civil rights legislation (after Andrew Johnson and Ronald Reagan), he gave half the profits from a book he wrote to the Negro College Fund. As a Texas congressman he risked his seat by voting for a Fair Housing Act, yet he ran a racist campaign for president in 1988, appealing to white fears of black criminals.

As president he appointed the first black chairman of the Joint Chiefs of Staff, Colin Powell, and a black Secretary of Health and Human Services, Louis L. Sullivan. Overall, however, black leaders saw his black appointments as politically motivated, not reflecting genuine concern for civil rights.

Receiving only 10 percent of the black vote in 1988, Bush was considered by 57 percent of both black and white newspapers in the 1991 *USA Today* poll to have done the least effective job of protecting civil rights. This judgment was confirmed by his cynical appointment of an ultra-conservative black judge, Clarence Thomas, to replace retiring black liberal Supreme Court Justice Thurgood Marshall. Thomas opposed affirmative action for blacks, though he himself had been admitted to Yale Law School only through that law. Almost all black congressmen opposed his nomination. His appointment was seen as a blatantly political move to bias further the already conservative Supreme Court stacked with Reagan and Bush appointees. Bush counted on Senate confirmation because he was sure the Senate would not dare turn down a black nominee for fear of being charged with racism.

Bush insisted that he had chosen Thomas as "the best

man for the job," but even White House aides agreed with Harvard law professor Christopher Edley that "if Thomas were white, he would not have been nominated." The NAACP opposed the nomination as an insult to the record of Justice Marshall.

The Senate confirmation hearing became a dramatic TV event when University of Oklahoma College of Law professor Anita Hill, a black woman, testified that she had been sexually harassed by Thomas years earlier, and produced witnesses to support her allegations. All her university colleagues vouched for Hill's integrity and honesty.

Thomas hotly denied Hill's charges against his character, calling them "a high-tech lynching for uppity blacks." Introducing the issue of racism, he ignored the fact that his accuser was also black. Republican committee members made brutal attacks on Hill's credibility, outraging millions of women watching on TV. The fourteen male senators then gave Thomas the benefit of the doubt and confirmed his appointment to the Supreme Court.

In 1989 the Supreme Court followed the Reagan-Bush line by attacking affirmative action programs, ruling that preference favoring blacks violated the civil rights of whites. The Court also shifted the burden of proof; companies no longer had to prove that they didn't discriminate, while employees who had less financial and legal resources had to prove they did. Further, the Court decreed that blacks could not sue state or local governments for discrimination, even when proven.

When the Democrats fought back by passing the Civil Rights Act of 1990, President Bush promptly vetoed it, charging that it would lead business to adopt quotas in hiring and promotion in order to avoid expensive lawsuits alleging discrimination.

Whites' fear of minority quotas was exploited in the 1990s. Senator Jesse Helms won reelection in North Carolina by running TV ads showing the hands of a white man crumpling a letter of rejection. The voice-over said, "You needed that job and were the best qualified. But they had to give it to a minority because of a racial quota. Is that really fair?" Democrats blasted Helms for this blatant appeal to racial prejudice.

In 1991 the Democrats reintroduced their Civil Rights Act, adding women and the handicapped to minorities who could sue for discrimination and expressly forbidding the use of quotas in hiring. As the NAACP's Benjamin L. Hooks noted, civil rights advocates accepted more than thirty changes to accommodate the White House. He told me, "We and our allies have always been prepared to accept reasonable changes in the legislation to make it abundantly clear it is not a quota bill."

Republicans prepared to use the racial issue against Democrats in the 1992 presidential and southern Senate races by continuing to brand the act as a quota bill discriminating against whites. President Bush again vetoed the bill.

Even Missouri's Republican senator, John C. Danforth, acknowledged that the message to whites, "You better watch out or the blacks are going to get your job," was "a Republican election ploy." He objected, "It's destructive for the country and not right for the Republican party to use that issue."

Blacks were dismayed in June 1992 when the Supreme Court struck down city ordinances banning "hate crimes" like burning crosses, swastika displays, and other expressions of racial supremacy and bias. The court voted 9–0 that these ordinances violated free speech rights. Blacks saw the decision as an invitation to the Ku Klux Klan and racial bigots to spread their acts of hatred free of the fear of prosecution.

Few blacks were happy with the Reagan-Bush Supreme Court of the nineties. Blacks also expected little from lower courts, where a large percentage of presiding judges were also appointed by the two Republican presidents. Disappointed with the administrations' favoring of business interests over individual rights, many blacks saw the white power structure in the federal government as slow and reluctant to help blacks solve their problems, but quick to respond to such pressures as farm subsidies for wealthy white ranchers and tobacco growers.

Instead of looking forward to further advances in the civil rights movement, black organizations now girded their loins to battle just to stop the gains already achieved from being eroded by the courts and the federal government.

T H R E E

B L A C K S have become increasingly involved in politics, both as voters and politicians. In 1988 the Reverend Jesse Jackson forged a Rainbow Coalition to organize black and white voters behind civil rights programs. He won the support of half of all young voters aged nineteen to twenty-four of both races and was responsible for over two million new voters entering the political process. In many cases they provided the margin for black election victories. Jackson's coalition was also credited with returning the Senate to the Democrats.

The number of black voters in the South increased by four million since the federal enforcement of voter registration. There are now over seventy-three hundred black elected officials, including mayors of several major cities, compared with only three hundred when the 1965 Voting Rights Act was passed. Even Birmingham, once a stronghold of Bull Connor racism, elected a black mayor, one of four in Alabama.

"I can remember back in 1968 when Andy Young and I were arrested in Atlanta for lying down in front of some garbage trucks during a strike," recalled the Reverend Joseph Lowery, president of the SCLC in the early 1980s. "Today Andy is the mayor of Atlanta and in charge of the garbage trucks."

Once the most racist state in the nation, Mississippi has undergone some remarkable changes. Over six hundred thousand blacks are now registered to vote, and do, resulting in six hundred black elected officials, more than in any other state. On the twenty-fifth anniversary of the 1964 murders of the three civil rights workers Schwerner, Chaney, and Goodman, their families went to Mississippi to commemorate their loss. They were accompanied by over a thousand former Freedom Riders.

"We deeply regret what happened here twenty-five years ago," Mississippi Secretary of State Richard Molpus told them. "We wish we could undo it. . . . Every decent person in Philadelphia and Neshoba County and Mississippi feels exactly that way. . . . It must never happen again." This was the state's first public recognition of past violent crimes against civil rights workers.

Yet next morning the letters KKK were painted in red two feet high across four downtown buildings.

One helpful sign of black political progress in jurisdictions with a white majority was the election of black politicians like Governor Douglas Wilder of Virginia, Mayor David Dinkins of New York City, and Mayor Tom Bradley of Los Angeles.

"We're seeing the emergence of what I call a New Black

Politics," said Howard University professor Ronald Walters. "These are black politicians who benefited from the civil rights movement. But they don't come out of it. They are the wave of the future, as more blacks run in white districts."

Jesse Jackson called this development "the maturing of white America." Most of the New Black Politicians won elections by moving to the political center, reassuring white voters that they were not black radicals concerned only about black issues.

Their election may also have represented a backlash by voters fed up with racist smear campaigns like the ones used by Helms to scare white voters about affirmative action, and by Bush to frighten them with allegations that Democrats release black criminals like Willie Horton to commit more crimes.

In 1992 three black candidates were even considered for a presidential ticket—Jesse Jackson, Governor Douglas Wilder, and General Colin Powell, chairman of the Joint Chiefs of Staff.

"While there are a number of African-Americans well qualified to be president," National Urban League president John E. Jacob told me, "I suspect the racial climate makes it very doubtful that a black candidate would be elected at this time."

Younger blacks today have no memory of the Democrat-led struggle for civil rights legislation in the 1960s and consequently do not feel the same bond to the Democrats their parents and grandparents do. The Republican party has wooed their votes by showcasing upwardly mobile young blacks who are making it in today's economy. But most blacks were turned off the Bush administration by the loss of jobs and job opportunities in the bleak recession of 1992. As a result, in the 1992 presidential election, the vast majority of blacks voted for Democrat Bill Clinton, who ran as "the candidate of change."

FOUR

IN 1991 inner city schools came under fire for doing a poor educational job, especially for black children. In the largest cities at least two out of five black children never graduate from high school. Black leaders complain that ghetto schools are too poorly equipped to do a good job.

"What do they expect our kids to be when they've never seen a test tube, let alone a science lab?" protested Chicago black parent Sheila Garrett. "My kids are damn well going to get what those other [white] kids get!"

According to the ACLU, some states, such as Kansas and Connecticut, still practice de facto school segregation, and blacks receive an education inferior to that given whites. In Hartford suburban schools are still 92 percent white, with less than one student in four coming from a poor family, and over 82 percent of these students score high in reading and math. But Hartford's inner city schools are 91 percent black and Latino, with over half the students from poor families, and over 70 percent scoring poorly in reading and math.

Black parents had high hopes back when the Supreme Court first ordered schools desegregated by busing. During the first ten years after busing began, black students' achievement scores climbed close to those of white students. Federal aid for remedial education programs helped compensate for the fact that poor black children generally started out farther behind.

But funds for those programs were cut drastically by the Reagan and Bush administrations. Black parents also blamed white teachers for a decline in their children's scores. Because those teachers often expected less of poor black students, their expectations became a self-fulfilling prophecy.

"Somebody's given up on us," said the Reverend Rudolph Seth, president of the Charlotte, North Carolina, branch of the SCLC.

One bright spot, however, has been the Head Start program begun by President Lyndon Johnson to put poor three- to five-year-olds in preschool to overcome disadvantaged backgrounds. Widely hailed for giving black youngsters the preparation they need to cope with traditional schooling, Head Start made it far less likely that they would drop out of school into delinquency.

But today only a small percent of eligible children benefit from Head Start for even one year. Congress tried to vote more funds to extend the program to cover all needy children, but the Bush administration opposed the bill as "excessive." The Clinton administration reintroduced the bill.

It is a sign of black discomfort at white institutions that enrollment at black public universities rose from 120,000 in 1987 to 160,000 in 1991. "Historically white colleges are not capable of addressing the needs of black students," declares Dolores R. Spikes, president of all-black Southern University in Louisiana, "because whites are socially and culturally deprived of understanding the needs, desires, abilities, and mores of black students."

Blacks have also been targets of hostility on many university campuses. In 1990 some right-wing college students, angry at what they considered favored treatment of blacks, formed White Student Unions to promote "white culture" and "white pride." These groups sprang up on as many as fifteen campuses across the country. They demanded an end to affirmative action and minority scholarships and protested curtailing Western studies to make room for teaching African culture and history.

Racist episodes were also reported at over three hundred colleges and universities from 1986 to 1991. At Yale ten black law students received death threat "Nigger" notes after a white student had been raped by an unknown assailant.

"The epidemic of racist incidents that has raged in recent years on college campuses has severely tested my faith. . . ." said the ACLU's Ira Glasser in the fall of 1990. "Too many young people feel it's legitimate to be openly racist. . . . The problem has moved to a new level now that white kids seem, suddenly, to feel *comfortable* yelling nigger, or harassing people on the basis of race."

Racial slurs often lead to violence. But attempts to prevent them on campus have led conservatives to accuse liberals of trying to enforce "politically correct" racial thinking. Banning inflammatory racist speech, they charged, would be a violation of the First Amendment.

Most liberals reluctantly agree, except when racist speech deliberately incites to violence. Lawyer Floyd Abrams argues, "Americans have made a brave and sophisticated choice" in deciding to endure hateful speech in the greater interest of free, vigorous political debate. Some believe that letting white racists spout their bigotry backfires by exposing their prejudice and fanatical hatred.

Today black athletes dominate collegiate and professional sports. A lot of black high school athletes are awarded college scholarships. Blacks constitute 36 percent of college football players and 52 percent of college basketball players. But only 14 percent of these athletes graduate. The rest are exploited to earn the colleges huge TV fees for broadcast games.

In the long run, the best hope of getting blacks to the level where affirmative action will no longer be necessary is better education. To make that happen, teachers need to make extra efforts to educate minorities. They need to be trained to care about, and expect good things from, black children. Children are more likely to try harder when they sense a teacher's confidence in them. Occasionally some black youngsters lift themselves up by their bootstraps even when not encouraged.

One New York City teacher told a black kid she thought a little slow that she wanted to place him with slower kids. That kid eventually turned out to be General Colin Powell, chairman of the Joint Chiefs of Staff.

We also need to restore federal aid for remedial education programs that help compensate for the fact that many black children start out farther behind white children. Larger funds will probably be appropriated for the highly successful Head Start program, which now reaches only one in six black children.

A fairer deal for black children in America's classrooms is the best way to assure them of decent opportunities in the workplace that can help them realize their hopes and dreams.

FIVE

WHILE there is less job discrimination today than in the past, a good deal still persists. When the Urban League sent pairs of equally qualified black and white youths to apply for 476 entry-level jobs, one of five times the black wasn't given a chance to apply while the white applicant was.

In 1991, even with J. Edgar Hoover long gone, the FBI had to be sued by black FBI agents who were being denied promotions.

The loss of black job opportunities has led to the absence

of husbands from black families, leaving many mothers with children on welfare. Years earlier, when three out of four black men were working, three out of four black families were intact.

With inflation jumping about 5 percent every year, most employed blacks earn from the minimum wage up to $7 an hour and are unable to meet the basic needs of their families. In 1987 the average white income was almost double that of blacks.

Black children who have to leave school early to help support their families have much less chance of climbing out of a bare ghetto existence themselves.

In 1991 and 1992 unemployment rose severely and many jobless whites protested affirmative action programs that required companies to bring millions of blacks into factories and offices that were once lily-white. Blacks represented almost one in ten teachers, over 18 percent of social workers, over 7 percent of accountants and auditors. There were also 799,000 black managers and executives, an increase of 293,000 in four years.

If whites complained about this growth of black competition, blacks complained that they had to be twice as good and work twice as hard just to be considered equal. But many whites believed that, after two decades of government-decreed affirmative action, enough had been done to rectify past injustices to blacks. They complained of "reverse discrimination"—losing jobs to less qualified blacks because of racial preference.

White bitterness was reflected by Chicago policeman Jim Cosgrove, who was finally made a sergeant in 1991 after nineteen years on the force. He claimed he had been passed over for promotion by as many as 150 black and female officers with lower performance scores. Originally a supporter of affirmative action, Cosgrove complained that "now it's gone overboard. Historic discrimination wasn't imposed by the people being passed over for promotion today. What did *I* have to do with slavery? Why is the little guy paying this cost?" Such white protests have made it much harder for liberal congress members to pass new civil rights legislation.

President Bush called the military "the greatest equal opportunity employer around." Blacks in West Point numbered no more than nine a year in the early 1970s. Since 1985 West Point has been enrolling up to a hundred blacks a year and in June 1991 graduated its one-thousandth black cadet. The military's antidiscrimination regulations have placed unprecedented numbers of black men and women in positions of authority unequaled in civilian life.

On the other hand, severe slashes in the defense budget in 1992 forced many blacks in uniform to leave the service. Those without adequate education were at a severe disadvantage in obtaining jobs in a depressed American economy.

To help black adults who are school dropouts, we need community colleges to provide reeducation for them, whether or not they even finished primary school. We will need all the educated workers we can get in the coming century.

Companies and universities have to work harder at recruiting and assisting blacks who may need help in handling requirements and catching up. To deny blacks job opportunities is to force them onto welfare rolls.

Welfare has constantly been a battleground between liberals and conservatives, the latter arguing that it should be abolished as a disincentive to work. Liberals insist instead that the minimum wage should be raised, with extended Medicaid benefits to working mothers, because otherwise they actually fare better on welfare. Many states now operate "workfare"—offering jobs or paid job training in place of welfare, with day care for the children of one-parent families.

Some successful blacks believe that more blacks could succeed if the jobless were only willing to take any jobs they could get and work hard. Joshua Smith founded the Maxima Corporation in 1979, today one of the ten largest black-owned businesses in the nation.

"I wouldn't trade my experience of cleaning floors and cooking," he declares, "because the kids who used to laugh at me are now the kids who want a job from me." He firmly believes in the work ethic as the best way out of the ghetto.

Shirley Chisholm, former congresswoman and chairperson of the National Association of Black Organizations, called on them to develop more black businesses to create more black jobs. She believed that blacks had to look more to themselves and less to the government to improve their standard of living. "We have to be accountable for the state of our race," she declared.

S I X

A S T U D Y by University of Chicago sociologists in 1988 found that little progress had been made in integrating housing in America. In California a proposition affirming the right of blacks to buy housing wherever they wished was placed on the ballot, but voters rejected it by a margin of two to one.

While middle-class black families still face housing discrimination, they have at least managed to escape the ghettos. Yet over half of all black families, many headed by desperately struggling women, remain behind in slums where the rate of unemployment for black youths and of teenage pregnancies are twice that of white young people. Run-down public housing projects inhabited almost entirely by blacks are often neglected. Renters are terrorized by gangs who rob, murder, rape, and push drugs. In one Chicago project, an average of eight crimes per one hundred residents have been recorded annually. Murder victims are often children.

The alarming rise in drug use during the 1980s and the possibility of making fast, easy money tempted many unemployed black and white youths to become street dealers. Drugs were the cause of many gun battles in the ghettos. Many ghetto children quickly learned the rules of survival. At home if they heard gunfire, they dropped to the floor. If they were on the street, they looked to see where the shots were coming from before running for cover.

"If I grow up," one fifteen-year-old Chicago black declared, "I'd like to be a bus driver." *If*, not *when*.

Black mayor Emanuel Cleaver of Kansas City, Missouri, who used to be a militant civil rights activist, believes that those years taught him the patience needed to struggle with the drug problem.

"Back then we thought our only opponent was bigotry," he recalled. "Now our most diabolical opponent is crack— crack and the crime that comes with it."

Still, bigotry and the racial violence that often accompanies it remain serious problems. Whites and blacks most often involved in racial violence have three things in common: poor education, no job skills, and bleak, depressing futures. "You are seeing what happens when the possibilities for low-income people are cut back," said Madeline Lee of the New York Foundation. "They turn on each other."

If whites grew nervous in the presence of groups of black youths, blacks became nervous on white "turf." Yusuf Hawkins, a sixteen-year-old black who ventured into the mostly

Italian Bensonhurst section of Brooklyn to buy a used car, was set upon by a gang of white youths who beat him with baseball bats before ending his life with two gunshots. This followed an attack on black youths by a white mob in the Howard Beach section of Queens, where one black was killed by a car after being forced to flee onto a highway.

Black New York mayor David Dinkins felt compelled to appeal for racial calm. "I oppose all bigotry against anyone, anywhere," he cried. "I abhor it. I denounce it, and I'll do anything—anything right and anything effective—to prevent it."

While poor whites turn on poor blacks, poor blacks turn against other ethnic groups—particularly Hispanics and Asian immigrants. Poor blacks resent them as rivals for jobs and economic advancement in small businesses.

"What they see are people who are not black," explains University of California sociologist Ivan Light, "who are soaking up economic opportunities that ought to be available to them. They seem people who are taking their money out of their neighborhood." Chicago Alderman Robert Shaw considered the real culprits to be not the immigrant businesspeople, but the banks who refuse loans to blacks wanting to start businesses.

Hostility between blacks and other ethnics has sometimes erupted in violent street battles. Miami blacks became especially embittered when Cuban refugees, who had gained political power in the city, gave favored treatment to new Nicaraguan refugees while neglecting the plight of Miami's poor blacks.

In Chicago, Brooklyn, and Philadelphia, blacks complained about neighborhood shops owned by Korean and Arab merchants, accusing them of being rude or treating blacks like shoplifters. Black rap singer Ice Cube warned Korean merchants, "Pay your respect to the black fist, or we'll burn your stores right down to a crisp!"

"I know black people look at us and see us succeed," observed Korean sociologist Yoon Lee, "and it only reminds them how far they are still behind. But you cannot blame Koreans or Arabs for that."

Nothing created a national uproar like that which occurred in October 1991 when black Rodney King was stopped by Los Angeles police after a high-speed chase. Dragged from the car by four policemen, he was beaten mercilessly and continuously with batons—over fifty blows inflicted as he lay helpless on the ground, offering no resistance. Even other officers simply stood aside and watched as the victim's skull was broken in nine places.

A bystander recorded the atrocity with a camcorder. His videotape was shown on national TV newscasts to millions of shocked Americans. A popular outcry led to the resignation of L.A. Police Chief Daryl Gates, whose stormy tenure had been marked by allegations of racism and brutality.

"Racism is widespread in the department," black L.A. officer Carl McGill charged. "There's racism in the hiring practices, racism in the employment practices. The department reflects the old days when blacks and other minorities were second-class citizens."

The Rodney King case sparked a demand that the Justice Department probe police brutality in all major cities. For many blacks, the Rodney King incident was simply the tip of the iceberg of police brutality, with a double standard of justice—one for blacks, one for whites.

The four policemen who had brutalized King were tried

in 1992 in Simi Valley, a middle-class white L.A. suburb, the bedroom community for many L.A. police. To the amazement and outrage of the millions who had watched the videotape of the beating, which was also shown to a jury of ten whites, one Hispanic, one Asian, and no blacks, the four officers were acquitted.

As soon as this incredible verdict was announced, infuriated mobs rampaged through the streets of Watts shouting for justice. In the deadliest riot in twenty-three years, Americans watched on TV as whole city blocks were set afire, car windows were smashed, and cars were torched while drivers fled for their lives. One white driver was pulled from his truck and savagely beaten by gang members. Flames and smoke engulfed the neighborhood. Police were nowhere in sight as the city went wild with rage.

Gangs, including Hispanics, took advantage of the riot to smash into stores and malls to loot. Over one hundred Korean-owned stores, targets of black resentment, were burned to the ground. Over forty people were killed and over seven thousand were arrested as violence raged for days. National Guard and Army units had to be called out to enforce a curfew and stop the rioting, which was even worse than the Watts riot of 1965.

Shocked city dwellers all over the country feared that mob violence would overwhelm them, too. There were outbreaks of violence and arson in Peoria, Atlanta, San Diego, New York, Denver, Bridgeport, Jersey City, and other cities, as well as peaceful protest demonstrations against the Rodney King verdict.

The uproar reached my area of California as well. San Francisco had to be placed under a curfew for two nights, and 1,500 demonstrators were arrested. In my city of Santa Cruz,

150 high school students protested by lying in the streets and blocking traffic, while a small number committed acts of vandalism.

After the riots, stormy debates took place in the media and in communities over their significance. Most Americans deplored the miscarriage of justice in the acquittal of the four police officers. At the same time they condemned the riots as the wrong way to protest.

But most Americans were shocked into a renewed recognition of the rage and mindless violence of the dispossessed poor in the ghettos. The riots were recognized as the cost of twenty-five years of societal and governmental neglect. As Martin Luther King, Jr., remarked about the race riots a quarter of a century earlier, "I condemn the violence of the riots, but I understand the conditions that cause them. I think we must be just as concerned about correcting those conditions as we are about punishing the guilty. . . . I seriously question the will and moral power of this nation to save itself."

Public outrage over the police trial verdict compelled the federal government to indict the officers in federal court for violation of Rodney King's civil rights.

There was now general agreement, even by the reluctant Bush administration, that the problem could no longer be ignored and that remedial action was urgently needed. Poor American blacks had to be given their share of the American dream. Congress hastily passed an emergency aid bill to provide summer jobs for black teenagers in rebuilding the Watts ghetto.

Black bitterness over police brutality became the theme of lyrics sung by rap singers, some of which seemed to urge blacks to kill cops. Black rap singer Sister Souljah created a storm of excitement by declaring in an interview with the *Washington Post*, "I mean, if black people kill black people every day, why not have a week and kill white people?" Democratic presidential candidate Bill Clinton denounced her in July 1992 as a racist.

To bridge the gap between black ghettos and white suburbs, we need programs that will encourage integration of large numbers of blacks into mainstream society. More, better regulated and maintained housing projects are required to place new low- and moderate-income housing outside the ghettos.

Until then, the plight of the ghettos needs immediate attention. One of the most urgent needs is a drastic improvement in relations between blacks and police. Crime and violence can only grow worse as an increasing youth population outstrips police resources to cope with it. Police need to be trained to treat blacks as nonviolently as possible. They also need training in how to intervene when they see another police officer breaking the law.

Significantly, other civilians have begun training their camcorders on police arrests of blacks since the Rodney King beating was videotaped, with far better results than when the Black Panthers tried to monitor police brutality by trailing police cars. The Panthers' strategy failed because it escalated tension, while the camcorder exposure of police brutality has succeeded by focusing media attention on the problem.

Some communities have introduced new programs that involve police in black children's social and athletic activities, to establish friendly relations as early as possible with youngsters and their parents. To make police an accepted, integral part of the community, many mayors are increasing the number of blacks on their police forces.

But black politicians have their work cut out for them to maintain and extend civil rights in the years ahead. The debate on civil rights has come full circle from the days when slavery was considered a "business issue." In the fifties and sixties, business interests were subordinated to issues of individual rights and equality. In the eighties and nineties, economic and business interests once more predominated over the rights of black individuals.

There will be no racial peace in America until the pendulum once again swings in favor of civil rights—and stays there.

SEVEN

ANY solution to the problems of inner-city blacks has to begin with changes in the attitudes of white America. If we are ever to achieve racial harmony, blacks and whites are going to have to communicate, and interact, much better than we do now.

"Few whites and minorities are friends," observed the ACLU's Ira Glasser in 1990. "They eat separately. They party separately. . . . Where are the programs to teach people how to respect differences, how to appreciate each other's contributions?"

"How long has it been," Senator Bill Bradley of New Jersey asked both blacks and whites bluntly, "since you had an honest conversation about race with someone of a different race? If the answer is never, you're part of the problem."

Whites need to be made more aware of racist feelings they harbor, consciously or unconsciously, stemming from their childhoods. As Gunnar Myrdal observed over half a century ago, "The social paradox in the North is . . . that almost everybody is against discrimination in general but, at the same time, almost everybody practices discrimination in his personal affairs."

When the races are able to spend more time together they will learn, according to black Harvard law professor Randall Kennedy, that "workaday black people's aims and understandings aren't very different from white America's."

Black leaders complain of TV newscasts that constantly feature arrests of blacks for street crimes, but cover few constructive black events. The blacks shown are usually violent youths to be feared and avoided, creating the impression that *all* young black American males are involved in drugs, robbery, mugging, rape, and murder. These images are destructive to black self-esteem and make some despairing young blacks feel that violence and social failure are their inescapable fates.

In actual fact, a 1991 *USA Today* poll showed that only 15 percent of drug users in America are black, while 70 percent are white. According to a *Black Entertainment News* study, however, TV news associates drugs with blacks 50 percent of the time, but only 32 percent of drug stories focus on whites.

Many blacks feel that neither TV nor the movies have done justice in portraying blacks who had put their lives on the line in the civil rights movement.

"The media does not credit blacks with doing enough," complains *Philadelphia Inquirer* columnist Claude Lewis. "In most instances it does not show the beauty and heroics of people who were dedicated to democracy."

One brilliant exception was the six-part public television series *Eyes on the Prize*, which depicted the moral courage and inspired leadership of civil rights crusaders in the face of terror. That series inspired today's black youths lucky enough to have seen it with a sense of racial pride and hope for the future.

Some successful blacks have sought to be public role models and mentors for ghetto youths. The Page Education Foundation, founded by Alan Page, former tackle with the Minnesota Vikings and now assistant attorney general of Minnesota, provides financial assistance to graduating black high school students.

"We require them," Page says, "to go back and work in the schools in the community to encourage and motivate young kids."

A Memphis organization called the One Hundred Black Men, composed of successful blacks, urges every middle-class black to "help just one boy become a man." They reach out to boys with problems, many of them fatherless, to serve as role models and father figures.

Eugene Rivers, a Harvard-educated black minister, moved his Radcliffe-educated wife and two children into a Dorchester, Massachusetts, ghetto to establish a home for black street kids. He hoped by example to influence other middle-class blacks to come into the ghetto to serve as role models and surrogate parents.

Many states are experimenting with school programs aimed at raising the self-esteem of black children, reflecting the efforts of Marcus Garvey and Malcolm X to instill blacks with more racial pride.

"Children are bombarded with messages from society," observes Connecticut psychologist Darlene Powell Hopson, "that give them the idea that there's something positive about white and negative about black. If students are made to feel uncomfortable, that they're not a part of the process, they feel alienated and it affects their ability to achieve and their motivation in school. . . . Work to make your children feel they are unique, yet equal to other children. This means taking pride in a black heritage of achievements, as well as in personal achievements."

Black students need and deserve to learn the contributions of blacks to American history. Yet high school librarian Byrl Graham of Boston points out that factual material on black women is sadly deficient in all encyclopedias for children.

"The varied ways that children are affected by biographical information," she explains, "cannot be overemphasized, and models are most important to them. Most children tend to relate to heroes and heroines where they find them."

More and more black educators are teaching black children about black Americans of achievement to give them a sense of racial pride and inspire them to achievements of their own.

The accomplishments of such political black trailblazers as Douglass, Garvey, King, Malcolm X, W. E. B. Du Bois, A. Philip Randolph, Mary McLeod Bethune, James Farmer, Ralph Bunche, Adam Clayton Powell, Thurgood Marshall, and Ralph Abernathy paved the way for Jesse Jackson, Tom Bradley, Shirley Chisholm, and Barbara Jordan.

Famous black writers like Langston Hughes, Richard Wright, and Ralph Ellison paved the way for James Baldwin, Alex Haley, Toni Morrison, and Alice Walker.

Famous black music and entertainment figures like Scott Joplin, Louis Armstrong, Count Basie, Paul Robeson, Duke Ellington, Cab Calloway, Mahalia Jackson, Sarah Vaughan, Ella Fitzgerald, Billie Holiday, Lena Horne, and Harry Belafonte paved the way for Bill Cosby, Sidney Poitier, Michael Jackson, Oprah Winfrey, Eddie Murphy, Whoopie Goldberg, James Earl Jones, Gregory Hines, Richard Pryor, Arsenio Hall, Stevie Wonder, and Spike Lee.

Famous black sports figures like Jack Johnson, Jesse

Owens, Sugar Ray Robinson, Joe Louis, Sugar Ray Leonard, Floyd Patterson, and Jackie Robinson paved the way for Muhammad Ali, Magic Johnson, Michael Jordan, Carl Lewis, Mike Tyson, George Foreman, and Kareem Abdul-Jabbar.

Opportunities for blacks have never been brighter in many fields. More and more black politicians are being elected in black and mixed communities. More and more books are being published by black authors and are receiving critical attention. More and more black actors are being seen on TV and in movie houses. And the number of blacks in sports like basketball, baseball, hockey, and boxing is increasing by leaps and bounds.

Frederick Douglass, Marcus Garvey, Martin Luther King, Jr., and Malcolm X overcame tremendous obstacles leading to the development of the civil rights movement. The remarkable success of that movement has made it possible for millions of blacks today to enter the middle class and live comfortable, creative, and productive lives, and for new, effective black leaders to emerge and carry the struggle further.

Their work will not be finished until the ghettos have been replaced by model communities and the whole problem of civil rights simply becomes ancient history, like abolition.

The heroic dedication of the pioneers of the civil rights movement in triumphing over racial barriers made it inevitable that some day during the twenty-first century or sooner, we will no longer have whites, blacks, Hispanics, and Asians in our country, but only Americans. Americans conscious of and proud of their racial heritages, yes, but living and working together as one harmonious national family.

And whenever we encounter discouraging setbacks today or tomorrow, we need to heed Jesse Jackson's rallying cry:

"Keep hope alive!"

BIBLIOGRAPHY
AND
SUGGESTED
FURTHER READING

(Suggested further reading indicated by *)

* Aptheker, Herbert. *A Documentary History of the Negro People.* New York: Citadel Press, 1965.
* Archer, Jules. *Angry Abolitionist: William Lloyd Garrison.* New York: Julian Messner, 1969.
* ———. *The Incredible Sixties: The Stormy Years That Changed America.* San Diego, New York, London: Harcourt Brace Jovanovich, 1986.
* ———. *1968: Year of Crisis.* New York: Julian Messner, 1971.
* ———. *Resistance.* Philadelphia: Macrae Smith, 1973.
* ———. *RIOT! A History of Mob Action in the United States.* New York: Hawthorn Books, 1974.
* ———. *Superspies: The Secret Side of Government.* New York: Delacorte Press, 1977.
    ———. *The Unpopular Ones.* New York: Crowell-Collier Press. London: Collier-Macmillan Limited, 1968.
    ———. *Who's Running Your Life? A Look at Young People's Rights.* New York and London: Harcourt Brace Jovanovich, 1979.
* ———. *Winners and Losers: How Elections Work in America.* San Diego, New York, London: Harcourt Brace Jovanovich, 1984.
* ———. *You and the Law.* New York and London: Harcourt Brace Jovanovich, 1978.
* Bishop, Jim. *The Days of Martin Luther King, Jr.* New York: Putnam's, 1971.
* Bontemps, Arna. *Frederick Douglass: Slave-Fighter-Freeman.* New York: Knopf, 1959.
    Breitman, George, ed. *Malcolm X Speaks.* New York: Grove Press, 1966.
    Breitman, George, and Herman Porter. *The Assassination of Malcolm X.* New York: Pathfinder Press, 1969.

* Breitman, George. *Malcolm X: The Man and His Ideas.* New York: Merit, 1965.

* Clark, John Henrik, and Amy Jacques Garvey. *Marcus Garvey and the Vision of Africa.* New York: Vintage Books, 1974.

Clayton, Ed. *Martin Luther King: The Peaceful Warrior.* Englewood Cliffs, NJ: Prentice-Hall, 1964.

* Cone, James H. *Martin and Malcolm and America.* Maryknoll, NY: Orbis Books, 1991.

Cronon, Edmund D. *Black Moses.* Madison, WI: University of Wisconsin Press, 1955.

* Dennis, Denice, and Susan Willmarth. *Black History for Beginners.* New York: Writers and Readers, 1984.

Douglass, Frederick. *Life and Times of Frederick Douglass.* New York: Crowell, 1966.

* ———. *Narrative of the Life of Frederick Douglass, An American Slave.* Benjamin Quarles, ed. Cambridge, MA: Belknap Press of Harvard University Press, 1967.

* Du Bois, W. E. B. *Black Reconstruction.* New York: Meridian Books, 1964.

* Fax, Elton C. *Garvey.* New York: Dodd, Mead, 1972.

Foner, Philip S. *Frederick Douglass.* New York: Citadel Press, 1964.

* Garvey, Amy Jacques. *Garvey and Garveyism.* New York: Collier Books, 1970.

* Garvey, Marcus. *Philosophy and Opinions of Marcus Garvey.* New York: Arno Press and The New York Times, 1968.

* Ginzburg, Ralph, ed. *100 Years of Lynching.* New York: Lancer, 1962.

Holland, Frederick Max. *Frederick Douglass: The Colored Orator.* Westport, CT: Negro Universities Press, 1891 (Reprinted 1970).

* Huggins, Nathan Irvin. *Slave and Citizen: The Life of Frederick Douglass.* Boston, Toronto: Little, Brown, 1980.

* King, Coretta Scott. *My Life with Martin Luther King, Jr.* New York, Chicago, San Francisco: Holt, Rinehart and Winston, 1969.

* Lewis, David L. *King: A Critical Biography.* New York, Washington: Praeger, 1970.

* Malcolm X. *Autobiography of Malcolm X.* Alex Haley, ed. New York: Grove Press, 1965.

* Miller, Douglas T. *Frederick Douglass and the Fight for Freedom.* New York, Oxford: Facts On File, 1988.

* Myrdal, Gunnar. *An American Dilemma.* New York: Pantheon, 1975.

* Osborne, Charles, ed. *I Have A Dream*. New York: Time-Life Books, 1968.
* Preston, Dickson J. *Young Frederick Douglass: The Maryland Years*. Baltimore, London: Johns Hopkins University Press, 1980.

Quarles, Benjamin. *Frederick Douglass*. New York: Atheneum, 1969.
* Rummel, Jack. *Malcolm X*. New York, Philadelphia: Chelsea House, 1989.

Schulke, Flip, and Penelope O. McPhee. *King Remembered*. New York, London: Norton, 1986.

Also consulted were articles in issues of *AARP Bulletin, ACLU News, ADL Special Report, AIM Quarterly, Civil Liberties, Essence, Good Times, The Historian: A Journal of History, Kansas City Journal, Los Angeles Daily News, The Nation, Newsweek, The New Yorker, The New York Times, The New York Times Magazine, Redwood Review, Santa Cruz Sentinel, School Library Journal, Time, USA Weekend,* and *Z Magazine*.

Interviews were held with Benjamin L. Hooks, former executive director of the NAACP; John J. Jacobs, President, National Urban League; Bobby Seale, cofounder of the Black Panthers; and David Hilliard, former chief of staff of the Black Panthers.

INDEX

About the Author

Jules Archer is one of the most respected names in non-fiction for young readers, with more than seventy books published. Intensive research and firsthand reporting are his hallmarks. Mr. Archer lives in Santa Cruz, California.